T0305078

OPTION MARKET MAKING

Wiley Finance Editions

OPTION MARKET MAKING

Trading and Risk Analysis for the Financial and Commodity Option Markets

ALLEN JAN BAIRD

John Wiley & Sons, Inc.

New York • Chichester • Brisbane • Toronto • Singapore

Copyright © 1993 by Allen Jan Baird
Published by John Wiley & Sons, Inc.
All rights reserved. Published simultaneously in Canada.

Library of Congress Cataloging-in-Publication Data:

Baird, Allen Jan.
    Option market making : trading and risk analysis for the financial
and commodity option markets / by Allen Jan Baird.
      p. cm. – (Wiley finance editions)
    Includes bibliographical references and index.
    ISBN 0–471-57832-0
    1. Commodity exchanges–United States. 2. Options (Finance)
United States. I. Title. II. Series.
HG6046.B32 1992
332.63'28–dc20   92-12010

10 9 8 7 6

Acknowledgments

I owe a debt of gratitude to the following people, who read all or parts of this book while it was still in manuscript and who generously offered helpful suggestions and encouragement that improved this book: James Meisner, Deene Lindsay, Norman Barta, Gary Gastineau, and Steve Weiss. Thanks are also due to Tom Bertolini, staff economist at the New York Cotton Exchange, who provided data for some of the figures in this book. Any errors and omissons are entirely my own.

I also owe special thanks to Wendy Grau, my editor at John Wiley & Sons, for shepherding this book through the editorial review and to Peter Feely, the production coordinator. I am gratefully indebted to my copyeditor, Marguerite Torrey, for all the many improvements in style and clarity and for the many questions that led to a better book.

Most of all I am grateful to my wife, Kathleen Hulser, who proofread early drafts of this book and who provided the patient and understanding atmosphere that allowed me to finish this book in a timely manner.

Preface

Since the introduction of stock option trading in 1974 and futures option trading in 1982, the total volume of option trading on all exchanges and over-the-counter markets in the United States is now billions of dollars a day. Option trading is one of the largest and most rapidly growing sectors of the financial industry. After a lag of about a decade, the option markets of Europe and Asia are following the growth path of the United States, promising that world option markets will become one of the most important sectors of the global financial industry in the 1990s and probably into the next century.

This book enumerates and evaluates the basic risks, strategies, and tactics of option market making as a profitable business. Its goal is to be both a theoretical and a practical reference for option traders, dealers, and market makers in financial and commodity option markets, whether they are trading on the exchange floor or in the growing national and international over-the-counter option markets.

Option market makers who will find this book of interest include dealers at banks and securities firms and trading members of option exchanges and over-the-counter markets. Interest rate managers in insurance and industrial corporations, investment officers of pensions, trusts, or funds, and option speculators should also find that knowledge of market making will improve their trading results or objectives.

The success of financial option markets requires the participation of many different traders: commercial hedgers, investment funds, speculators, and dealers or market makers. The functions of the first three are well known, but the role of the option dealer or market maker has not been widely researched, even though on a daily basis market maker trading volume is about half of all option trading. There are many good books about option trading but few, if any, exclusively address option market making.[1]

---

[1]Although there have been no books previously published about option market making, recently several introductory articles or chapters in books dealing briefly with this topic have appeared (CBOE, 1990; Colburn, 1990; Silber, 1988).

With a lack of good materials about this trading activity, option market makers learn their trading skills either from their employers or partners if they are lucky, or by trial and error, usually losing money in the process.

In the hope of making "paying one's dues" less costly for new traders, this book offers for the first time a comprehensive reference exclusively devoted to option market making in the commodity, bond, stock and currency option markets. Particular attention is given to futures options markets.

The function of market makers is to offer the service of *immediacy,* by always being willing to buy or sell for some quantity any option at some specified price. Thus, they provide liquidity and stability to the option markets. In return for liquidity and stability, market makers try to earn as income the difference in the price spread between bid and offer at which they will trade. In this respect, the profit function of market making is like any business in which merchandise must sell at a higher price than the cost of acquisition; but there are specific business risks to market making that must be thoroughly understood. Successful market makers may earn a high income as a percentage of capital invested, if a large turnover with low or containable risk can be assured. Because of the close relationship between risk and income, option risks and how they are managed are at the heart of profitability and success in market making.

The author is a professional option market maker on a futures option exchange, and this book largely stems from this professional experience. Professional floor traders generally content themselves with trading rather than writing. Indeed, publicizing trade secrets may be viewed as a self-defeating endeavor. There is probably some truth in this observation. Nevertheless, publicizing trade secrets will probably not change the fundamental profitability of option market making nearly so much as one might imagine. In any case, trade secrets rarely remain permanently secret.

STRUCTURE OF THIS BOOK

Chapters 1 and **2** provide an overview of the economics of market making and review option basics and terminology. Although the reader should have previously read at least one elementary book about options, some review of basic option definitions and theory is given here. This includes an introduction to fair value models, volatility, and some important differences between commodity, bond, currency and stock options markets.

Chapter 3 formally takes up the question of option risks and how they are to be measured. Trading options involves far more risks than other investments, and more complex risks at that. All option traders must be alert to the variety of these risks in daily trading. These risks are defined and summarized.

Chapter 4 explores different possible option strategies and the various risks in single-month option trades. It is always important to know the risk profile of any option position so that one can distinguish between those that risk financial catastrophe and those that promise safe and secure profits. Ignorance of risk may lead to financial ruin or sharp setbacks in trading as well as market making.

Chapter 5 discusses option market making from the perspective of synthetic option trading. This form of market making is virtually risk-free and represents the core of option arbitrage trading. Mastering synthetic price relations is essential for good scalping profits.

Chapter 6 systematically addresses the question of calendar spread risk and strategy. Understanding time risks is essential if one is to avoid the possibility of a catastrophic loss of market maker or public trading capital. Core market making trading strategy comes out of understanding how to limit time spread risk but still use time markets efficiently.

Chapter 7 discusses the overall strategic considerations in nonsynthetic market making from several perspectives. Topics include delta neutrality, neutral time spreading, broker order flows and net supply and demand, trading fences, and managing option cycle expirations. Detailed attention is given to the butterfly/ratio time spread strategy under different market conditions.

Chapter 8 takes up certain practical matters and tactics in making option markets in an active trading environment. Making a spread market, risk adjustment, gamma trading, implied volatility, skew, tracking, financial results, and avoiding mistakes are some of the topics.

Chapter 9 includes some personal observations about floor trading as a business and social experience.

Option market makers almost always use some option software to keep track of and analyze their option positions while trading. The reader does not need such software to understand this book, but active traders will almost certainly use option software. An appendix provides recent software information on option market making.

Contents

OPTION MARKET MAKING

1

Economics of Option Market Making

This study describes and evaluates the risks and opportunities in option trading from the standpoint of the professional option market maker. A market maker is a trader of options or any other liquid financial asset who is willing and ready at any time to buy at a bid price or sell at an offer price whatever is being traded. Market makers may also be known as dealers, especially in the securities, bond and currency over-the-counter markets, and sometimes as scalpers, when both the buy and sell sides of the trade are expected to be completed within a very short time. In stock and stock index option markets, market makers are institutionalized in the specialist system, but in futures options markets, market makers are independent traders in open competition.

A market maker provides a ready and liquid market for publicly brokered orders and, thus, the service of immediacy. The flow of buy-and-sell orders is rarely evenly matched at any given time, so without market makers prices would become more volatile and erratic as commercial and public buy-and-sell orders would become imbalanced (that is, another trader would not be willing to assume the opposite risk at that moment). By stepping into the market to meet the otherwise unfilled orders, market makers help bring prices back to a fair-value level that more accurately reflects the true supply/demand equilibrium. Market makers do not set prices (these are determined by more fundamental factors affecting supply and demand), but they do reduce price volatility, assuring the public of better and more accurate prices while trading in open markets. Market-making dealers are found on all financial, futures, and

1

over-the-counter option markets and are probably essential to the functioning of any open and fair market in which liquidity is important.

The above market situation may easily be reflected with the elementary supply/demand curve shown in Figure 1.1. Consider a situation in which a long-term equilibrium price is established at P* for some tradable financial asset. If a temporary imbalance of demand pushes the price to P1 or higher, market makers may be expected to enter the market and offer for sale a sufficient quantity to bring prices back to equilibrium. Likewise, if prices were to fall temporarily to P2 because of an imbalance between public buyers and sellers, market makers may be expected to enter the market and buy sufficient quantities to bring prices up to long-term equilibrium. At some level prices P1 and P2 around the equilibrium price will become the *asked* and *bid* prices at which a market maker is willing to trade. A more complete supply/demand analysis of market-maker services for stocks and a review of previous work may be found in Stoll (1987).

For every buyer or seller of options (or futures), there is an opposing seller or buyer. A long option holder is always paired with a short option seller (or writer). Thus, on a single option or futures contract, what one trader makes in profit the other must lose. Considering the option and futures market only, option and futures trading is a zero-sum game. Futures and futures option exchange trading neither adds nor subtracts from total wealth directly but shifts it from one group to another.

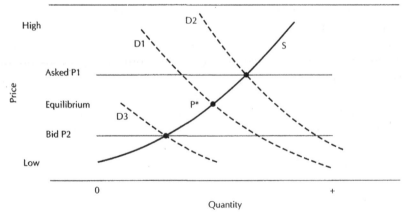

Figure 1.1   Dealer price.

Economic activity that leaves total wealth unaltered or merely shifts existing wealth is not necessarily useless or harmful, however. Insurance, for example, does not directly create wealth; but it provides a socially useful service of diversifying and shifting the risk of large and unexpected losses from one group to another. It is this risk-shifting and insurance function that futures and options markets provide to industry.

As an example, commercial firms, free of commodity price change risk with hedged futures, can concentrate on productive economic activity more rationally, and thereby increase total wealth. Although futures and options trading do not directly add to or subtract from total wealth, they provide a price insurance service to primary product producers and industrial consumers, thus increasing productivity and thereby total wealth.

Within the risk perspective of futures markets, options on futures represent the extension of risk shifting opportunity for futures speculators. With options, a speculator or hedger may insure or hedge his or her own futures holdings, either to lock in profits or to hedge against adverse futures price movements. Options are forms of risk shifting for the futures market itself. They are one way for commercial hedgers or speculators to insure their own futures risk.

For futures markets to perform price discovery and risk shifting functions successfully, futures market participants must include other market traders in addition to commercial hedgers. These traders are scalpers, market makers, and speculators. Scalpers and market makers assume that portion of risk that commercial hedgers or speculators wish to shift temporarily, but eventually wish to neutralize. Speculators ultimately assume the risk that commercial hedgers and market makers do not want. In effect, market makers and speculators distribute the unwanted investment risk of commercial hedgers and perform an insurance function to industry.

For providing a service of immediacy and liquidity, of course, a market maker expects to earn some profit from the difference between the temporary disequilibrium price and the long-term equilibrium price. By buying at the bid price and selling above long-term equilibrium at the asked price, the market maker earns this difference as profit for providing liquidity service. Buying low and selling higher is the cost framework of any business, and in exchange-floor terminology, this is known as "getting the edge."

Getting the edge is very important because, all else being equal, the market maker earns this price spread as income and profit. When a trader earns both sides of the edge on one contract, the trade is liquidated. Studies of securities dealers and futures scalpers suggest that the market makers are unlikely to earn the entire bid/offer spread as net profit on every trade, and this fact is true for option market makers as well (Working, 1977; and Silber, 1984 and 1988). There are certainly costs and risks to market making that reduce gross profits. As exchange members or over-the-counter dealers, market makers pay very low trading or brokerage fees; but they also must pay other overhead charges against memberships, office space, clerical and data services, and other business costs. Trading is not entirely cost-free even for market makers, and gross profits of the price spread will thus be reduced. The minimum price spread at which a market maker may expect to make a profit is known as the *reservation price.*

The difference between getting the edge and the reservation price represents the reduced gross profit, but even this is not necessarily net profit. Market making is not risk-free by any means. In earning a liquidity function income, market makers, dealers, and scalpers are exposed to the risk of windfall loss. The obvious risk to any scalper is that he or she will not be able to complete both sides of a bid/offer spread fast enough to earn more than the reservation price. A scalper may buy at the bid price but be unable to sell at the offer price. If the scalper sells the contract to another trader or broker at the same bid price at which the scalper bought the contract, the scalper would break even ("scratch the trade").

If the scalper was able to buy at his or her bid price, but unable to sell at either the original offer or the reservation price, then the scalper incurs an outright loss. Of course, in the interval between buying at the bid price and selling at the offer price, prices could rise, giving the scalper a windfall profit greater than the difference in the original bid/offer spread. This element of investment risk negates any guarantee that market making will be profitable as a business.

To maximize profits, market makers ideally would like to make the bid/asked dealer spread as wide as possible, but the dealer spread will be influenced by the demand for liquidity services and the supply of service or competition among market makers. The more actively traded the market and the greater the number of market makers, the narrower the dealer spread. In highly saturated markets, the presence of too many market makers will quickly narrow the dealer spread to the reservation price itself, in which case very little profit is earned by market making. Of course, this competitiveness among market makers gives broker orders the best possible price of execution. Indeed, to gain the edge on one trade, a market maker will often give up the edge in another trade, resulting in broker orders getting filled at better than equilibrium price to the benefit of the public trader.

Although the dollar profit on any individual trade may be small and usually is accompanied by numerous scratch or small-loss trades, the cumulative earnings from market making may become large in high- and active-volume markets when market making is done well. Of course, scalpers must always face the possibility of windfall losses as well as profits. Market making is not risk-free, and much market-making trading strategy is directed to investment risk control.

Differences in the degree of risk between dealing in securities, bonds, currencies, or futures markets and in option market making tend to affect dealer prices somewhat differently in option markets than in other asset markets. One difference between options and assets scalping, for example, is that market instrument liquidity in options trading is lower than in trading of other financial assets.

Stocks, currencies, and bonds are single-asset instruments, whereas there is no one option that matches the underlying risks of those assets. The multitude of strikes and calendar series (as defined in Chapter 2) in which options trade may easily push the distinct options traded into the hundreds for each underlying instrument, many of which may not trade on a regular basis. While an underlying-asset market maker is always a scalper on a short-term basis, this observation is not necessarily true of options market makers.

Although some near-term, near-strike options may trade in active markets almost as frequently as futures contracts, many options by month or strike may trade only infrequently. Thus, the market maker may end up owning or shorting contracts that he or she must be prepared to hold for long periods of time (even to expiration) unless he or she wishes to liquidate to other market makers, thus giving up the edge. Almost invariably, therefore, options scalpers must assume carryover positions on a regular basis, something a futures scalper does not do. It is a rare option market maker who is able to go home at the end of the day completely flat without overnight positions. Option market makers assume a large carryover risk that other financial dealers may not, and this longer-term assumption of risk may affect dealer price.

Option risk is more complex than many other investment risks. In assuming long-term risk exposure in the option market, market makers must be careful to understand exactly what these risks are. Options are highly leveraged instruments that do not always move in value dollar for dollar exactly corresponding to a futures or cash asset price change. The values of options characteristically shrink or explode at rapidly changing and sometimes greater rates than the underlying instrument. Options tend to decline in value over time (all else being equal), but option prices can also increase dramatically even without any time passing or change in futures price at all.

In being forced to hold long-term carryover positions in options, and thereby in being exposed to some long-term complex investment risks, market makers may lose in carryover positions what they make in liquidity function profits. In the worst case, a market maker can lose his or her entire capital. The 1980s witnessed perhaps half a dozen well-publicized multimillion dollar bankruptcies of large option traders, including two commodity exchange clearing houses—Volume Investors and Fossett (*The Wall Street Journal*, Oct. 13, 1987, and Michael Siconolfi, Nov. 12, 1990; *The New York Times*, Oct. 18, 1989). Although these bankruptcies were not necessarily those of option market makers, they clearly demonstrate the potential risks of option trading by the unwary and uninformed.

In attempting to earn a $10 liquidity function profit, option scalpers risk watching their long inventory go to zero and their short inventory rise to stratospheric prices in short order. This possibility represents catastrophic loss and is the most serious risk to any option trader. Floor traders who go bankrupt, or "blow out," trading options are a grim reminder that there are no easy profits in option trading.

An option market maker must always be prepared to "marry an option" (that is, to hold a long-term option position without liquidation or getting out), even as he or she strives to make a liquidity function profit on the transaction without taking undue risk. Since the chief risk is the possibility of financial catastrophe in the option carryover position, much of the skill in option market making comes from being able to manage these additional risks well in a large carryover position until expiration.

The perspective of this study is pure market making, where income comes solely from market making and not from speculative gain (or loss). Market-making, risk-neutral trading goals are to make a profit, not to be proved right about market direction.

To develop a prudent option market-making strategy, one must understand catastrophic option risk and establish practical measures to avoid this exposure; otherwise, one risks bankruptcy over the long run. Fortunately, not all option trading positions are catastrophically risk exposed, and some are limited-risk strategies. Limited-risk strategies for option market makers are not only safer than other option strategies, but also they are often safer than trading in the underlying asset itself. Knowledge of risk is the key to market-making option strategy.

Limited-risk strategy does not mean limited profits. Many low-risk strategies will also earn among the highest possible rates of return of any option strategy. Although market making as an economic activity earns an income for providing market liquidity, it is also possible to make option markets that sometimes earn large profits from time to time on the carryover position in windfall situations.

2

Options

WHAT IS AN OPTION?

A call (put) option is the contract right to buy (sell) a specified amount of some real or financial asset at a fixed price on or before a given date.

If the option purchaser acts upon this right to buy, he or she is *exercising* this right; and the fixed price of the transaction is known as the *strike* price. The seller of the option, known as the *writer,* must be prepared to sell the specified asset when the option purchaser exercises these rights. When the option buyer exercises, the seller is *assigned.* The *maturity* of the contract is known as the *expiration* date, and exchange option trading takes place in any one of a number of set contract months, or *cycles.* An *American* option allows the holder to exercise the right any time before the expiration, and a *European* option restricts the right only to expiration and not before.

A call is *in the money* at expiration when its asset price is above the exercise price, and a put is in the money when the asset price is below the exercise price. A call is *out of the money* at expiration when its asset price is below the exercise price, and a put is out of the money when the asset price is above the exercise price. Options in the money have real value, and those out of the money have no remaining value at expiration. An option is *at the money* when the asset price expires or trades right at the strike.

The underlying *asset* may be either the cash market (spot) or futures contracts on the underlying spot instrument (stocks, bonds, currency, or spot commodities). The spot option market holds a right to exercise over the cash asset itself. The futures option is on the futures contract only, which is then a right to delivery of the spot instrument. There may be both a cash and a futures option market trading in the same asset market, in which case cash/futures option arbitration will become important, whether in the stock, bond, and currency futures or over-the-counter markets.

The gross profit/loss (P/L), or expiration, payoff of a $100 strike call and put is illustrated graphically in Figures 2.1 and 2.2, where the purchase or trade price of both the put and call is $1.70. The 100 call allows the long holder to exercise the right to buy the underlying asset at $100 on (or sometimes before) expiration, and the short call writer must fulfill this demand. The 100 put allows the long holder to sell the asset at $100 to the short put writer on or before expiration.

Profit/loss is based on the expiration value of the option minus its trade price. If the asset settles at expiration at $102, for example, the long 100 call will expire in-the-money valued at $2.00 for a profit of 30 cents ($2.00 − 1.70) and a 30-cent loss for the short call. At an asset price of $110 at expiration, the call will be worth $10.00, for a net profit of $8.30 for the long call and a loss of $8.30 for the short call. The breakeven point for both the long and short call is an asset price of $101.70 at expiration, based on the trade

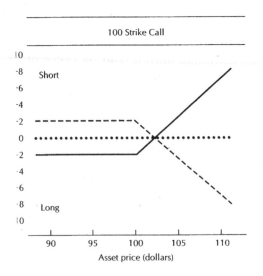

Figure 2.1 Payoff for long/short 100 strike options at expirations.

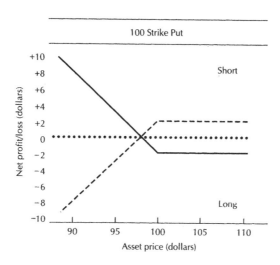

Figure 2.2 Payoff for long/short 100 strike options at expirations.

price of the option at $1.70. Below this asset value the long call will show a maximum loss of $1.70, and the short call will show a maximum profit of $1.70.

The breakeven point for the long or short 100 put will be an asset price of $98.30 at expiration, above which the long put will have a maximum loss of $1.70 and the short call a maximum profit of $1.70. Below the breakeven point, the long put will show increasing profit and the short call increasing losses.

While determination of the value of an option at expiration is relatively straightforward, its value before expiration is unknown. How much should an option be worth, or what is its fair value, before expiration? Clearly, it must equal at least the immediate exercise in- or out-of-the-money value or else an arbitrage profit generally becomes available, forcing price and value back in line. But how much more should be added above the in-the-money value to determine the fair value?

An options price depends on both the *intrinsic* and the *extrinsic* value of the option. The intrinsic value of an option is simply the value of the option if it were exercised immediately for cash value. The intrinsic value is always known and is a simple function of the relationship between asset price and the option strike. If the asset price is below the strike price of a call, the call will have no intrinsic value; and if the asset price is above the strike of the call, then the intrinsic value is the positive difference between the asset price and the strike. Puts have intrinsic value if the asset price is below the strike, but no intrinsic value if the price is above the strike. Options that have positive intrinsic value are in the money, and those without intrinsic value are out of the money.

For example, if a May future is at $110, then the 100 May call will be in the money and will be worth exactly $10 in intrinsic value, because a trader can exercise his or her long call rights to buy futures at $100 and immediately sell them for $110 on the open market. If futures are selling below $100, however, the 100 call will have no intrinsic value and will expire with no worth if this relationship holds until expiration. At expiration an option will be worth exactly its intrinsic value.

Whether a position has a net profit at expiration will, of course, depend on what the trader paid for the call. Only if the trader bought the call for less than $10 will there be a net profit if the futures price is at or above 110 at expiration. If the futures price closes below 100, however, the trader will lose money no matter what he or she paid for the 100 call.

In theory, the intrinsic value of an option will always set the minimum price that an option must have, since if it fell below that value, an arbitrage profit for market makers would quickly close the gap. Although option prices are limited on the downside by their intrinsic value, in practice, they usually trade above this value as long as there is time remaining to expiration.

Remaining time to expiration will add some additional value to an option's intrinsic value, which is known as the extrinsic value or time premium. Generally, the longer the time remaining, the higher the time premium. This valuation makes intuitive sense since a longer time remains for the option to become intrinsic-value profitable and, therefore, the option must be more valuable than at expiration.

Although the intrinsic value of an option is a direct function of futures or asset prices, it is the addition of extrinsic value or time premium that sets the total value of an option. Option valuation is essentially time premium pricing. How does the market set the price of the extrinsic value of options? How much should the time premium of an option be worth? Answers to these questions will be developed in the next section.

OPTION FAIR VALUE

An option may be considered fairly valued when it is priced so that trading at that price will produce neither gain nor loss over the long run, whether trading from the long or the short side. It is fairly valued because each side of the trade has equal economic advantage. When options are fairly valued in the market, they are best able to shift risk away from the underlying asset market. Acting essentially as an insurance factor to the underlying asset market, market makers in options must evaluate the risks of price changes carefully in order to charge an appropriate price for the insurance. How should options be fairly priced?

Modern fair-value option models, based on statistical models of probability, attempt to provide the answer to this question. The worth of an option is related to how likely it is to earn a profit or loss. To know fair value, however, requires a trader to know the probability of gain and loss for any specific option and, therefore, the probable future underlying asset price as well.

Before modern fair-value options models were developed, no theoretical model of option pricing could successfully generate hypothetical fair values of option time premiums. The price risk exposure of an option contract was evaluated subjectively, with only past empirical price and time relations somewhat imperfectly known. One can still value options in a relative way without a fair-value model if one knows the fixed arbitrageable synthetic price relations between puts, calls, and futures or asset prices (see Chapter 5). But synthetic option price relations do not establish a model of fixed absolute levels, that is, fair value itself.

Modern stock option pricing theory dates from the early statistical models of option premiums, especially the work of Fischer Black and Myron Scholes (1973), which was modified by Robert Merton (1973) into the BSM model. This model was adapted to commodity futures options by Fischer Black. The BSM model quickly came to be the most widely recognized and used stock and futures option value model; and it provides the statistical basis of this study, although alternative models will also be discussed for bond markets.

To understand how options are fairly valued statistically, let us review the probability of any kind of payoff-game outcome. As an example, consider a game in which, after a trial of only one period, there are only two possible outcomes, say heads or tails, with one outcome counting as a win and the other as a loss. Suppose a win results in a reward of $5, and a loss results in no reward, or $0. If the probability of either a win or a loss on one trial is 50 percent, what bet will neither gain to nor lose money if this game is played again and again? The answer to what a fair-valued bet should be is the probability of outcomes times the payoff, summed, or .50 × $0 + .50 × $5 = $2.50. Out of every two trials, there will be a total gain of just $5 on average (one win and one loss, or $5 + $0). Since it takes two trials on average to win $5, each bet must be $2.50 in order neither to win nor to lose money over a two-trial run over many plays.

The general formula for the fair value of a bet over a one-period trial, then, is the probability payoff schedule:

$$V = \sum (P) \cdot (\$)$$

where V = value of fair-value bet

P = probability of outcome

$\$$ = outcome payoff

Now consider a game in which there is only a one-period trial and for which the outcome values are either 105 or 95. Assume that an outcome of 105 will bring a profit of $5 and an outcome of 95, $0. Assume also that the probability of 105 or 95 occurring is exactly 50 percent on each trial. What is the value of a bet that will produce neither a profit nor a loss over the long run?

It may be seen that the answer again is exactly $2.50. Both games just described represent a one-event, binomial distribution with identical outcome payoffs and event probabilities. Calling a win heads, or 105, and a loss tails, or 95, does not change the essential similarity of the two games in any way. In each case, the bet that will produce neither a win nor a loss is calculated as the sum of the individual outcome probabilities times the outcome payoff, that is, .50 × $0 + .50 × $5 = $2.50.

Observe that the bet in the second game is equivalent to an investment or purchase of a hypothetical 100 call that can take only an exercise value of either 95 or 105 over a single period. By using elementary probability theory, one may calculate the fair value of a call option under these restricted specifications.

Now consider the possibility that outcomes are distributed within a range of 95 to 105 in one-point increments (that is, 95, 96,..., 105) and that the gain on each outcome is $0 at or below 100, and the numerical outcome less $100 when above 100; for example, 95 = $0, 96 = $0,..., 103 = $3, 104 = $4, 105 = $5. This result is similar to the payoff schedule of a hypothetical 100 call taken over a one-trial event.

If the probabilities of the specific outcomes are known, then, as in the previous examples, it is possible to calculate that fair-value investment or bet that will produce neither profit nor loss in the long run. For sake of illustration, assume that the outcomes from 95 to 105 have the following probabilities of occurring over a one period trial:

Possible Outcomes	Probability of Occurring (percent)
95	2
96	4
97	8
98	12
99	14
100	20
101	14
102	12
103	8
104	4
105	2

These probabilities are graphed in Figure 2.3, where the mean strike is 100.

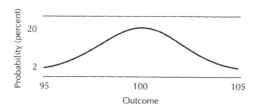

Figure 2.3   Outcome probability.

Since the specific payoffs as well as the probability for each outcome are known, the fair value of a bet may be determined exactly as in the previous games. That is, one multiplies the probability of an outcome by its expected payoff and sums the results to find the exact fair-value bet or investment. Thus,

Outcome 95	$0 × .02 =	$0
Outcome 96	$0 × .04 =	0
Outcome 97	$0 × .08 =	0
Outcome 98	$0 × .12 =	0
Outcome 99	$0 × .14 =	0
Outcome 100	$0 × .20 =	0
Outcome 101	$1 × .14 =	0.14
Outcome 102	$2 × .12 =	0.24
Outcome 103	$3 × .08 =	0.24
Outcome 104	$4 × .04 =	0.16
Outcome 105	$5 × .02 =	0.10
	Sum =	$0.88

Summing the expected payoffs gives a result of 88 cents, which represents the fair-value bet in this example, that is, that investment that neither wins nor loses repeatedly on one-period trials over the long run.

In the above example, one readily sees that the payoff schedule of each outcome (before the probability is taken into account) is just the payoff schedule of a hypothetical 100 call at expiration, or its intrinsic value from 95 to 105. Therefore, the only unknown in calculating the fair-value of such an option is the specific probability of each outcome. In other words, once the probability of outcome for an option's intrinsic value over some trial period is known, that option's fair-value price can be determined exactly.

In the preceding examples, we have assumed that the probability of outcomes is known exactly. But in the real world, the exact probability of occurrence for any specific intrinsic value of an option at expiration is not known directly. How, then, is it possible to derive such outcome probabilities for option analysis? How can we know what the probabilities are for the payoff of a hypothetical 100 call from 95 to 105, or from 50 to 150? The answers to these questions will be discussed in the next section.

OPTION PRICING MODELS

The key element of any option fair-value model is the probability assumptions about changes in underlying asset prices. If the probability distributions of asset price changes are known or can be successfully estimated, then these may be used to derive the probability densities of the expected payoff schedule of options at expiration, from which fair value may be derived.

More generally, if it is theoretically known that an asset price has an x percent chance of increasing by y points or more over the next z days, then an option price will be related to the outcome of this price change probability. A fair-value option price only reflects the intrinsic value at expiration, which is linked to the probability of underlying asset price change. If the distribution of futures prices is accurately estimated, so too will be the fair value of the option.

The probability of asset price change is usually referred to as *volatility* by option traders, and it is usually unknown. As a consequence, volatility must be estimated. Doing so gives rise to a number of different option pricing models.

Two other statistical assumptions or unknowns must also be incorporated in order to derive fair value for any model. (1) The risk-free interest rate must be known or estimated over the life of the option; and, (2) if the option is on a yield-bearing asset, the dividend or yield must be known or estimated over the life of the option. For bond options in particular, additional estimates of the term structure of interest rates may also be necessary. This chapter will review the Black-Scholes-Merton (BSM) option pricing model, but we shall also discuss some recent work in lattice-based and advanced bond option models.

The work of Black and Scholes in 1973, followed quickly by that of Merton the same year, proposed to link the probability of stock price changes to stock options using a log-normal distribution as the probability estimator. The BSM model was based on earlier statistical work that had shown that stock price changes could be modeled on a normal or Gaussian curve (Cootner, 1964). That is, futures (and stock) price changes resemble a random sample drawn from a universe that can be described by a log-normally distributed curve.

The finding that stock and asset price changes resemble known probability distributions makes it possible to develop theoretical models of price changes. The earliest fair value model of Black and Scholes used the normal-curve model of futures prices to derive option prices. The BSM model deduces option prices on the basis of statistical theory and thus supercedes subjective or graphical option price valuation. For example, the Fischer Black (1976) formula for European futures option fair value is:

$$C = e^{-rt}[XN(d_1) - KN(d_2)] \tag{1}$$

$$P = e^{-rt}[KN(-d_2) - XN(-d_1)] \tag{2}$$

$$d_1 = \frac{\ln(X/K) + (S^2/2)t}{S[t]^{1/2}} \tag{3}$$

$$d_2 = d_1 - S[t]^{1/2} \tag{4}$$

where $N(d)$ = cumulative normal integral

    r = risk-free interest rate

    S = standard deviation of log percentage change in annualized prices

    X = futures price

    K = strike price

    t = time to expiration, annualized

    C = call premium

    P = put premium

    e = exponent (2.7183)

    $\ln$ = natural logarithm

The BSM model requires information on five independent variables in order to estimate fair value for a non–income-earning future option:

1. The current futures price

2. Option strike price

3. Days to expiration

4. Risk-free interest rate

5. Standard deviation of futures price change or volatility

The current futures price is an empirical approximation of the mean of the normal curve; it is necessary in order to center the probability distribution. The option strike price represents our interest in a specific futures price outcome along the normal curve. Days to expiration, or the number of trial periods, is the empirical case frequency (or number of trial events) of the distribution. Calendar days are used in the BSM model rather than trading days. The risk-free interest rate is the opportunity cost of capital; it is taken to be the Treasury bill or note for the appropriate term of the option. Finally, volatility is the estimated standard deviation of futures price change over the number of trial periods, expressed as a logarithm. Volatility represents the probability of outcome of futures prices. To convert equation (1) for use with income-earning assets (for example, stocks, bonds, or currencies), one would need to subtract an expected future yield from the expected futures price. Colburn (1990:157–158), and Labuszewski and Sinquefield (1985:117–119), have presented empirical examples of the BSM formula.

Unfortunately, there is some evidence that the assumption of log-normality for financial and commodity asset price change may be inaccurate. Records in the stock and commodity markets over many years appear to show that financial asset price changes have a higher cental tendency with longer tails than the theory of normality would suggest (Cootner, 1964; Brealey, 1969; Turner and Weigel, 1990; Sterge, 1989; Nelson, 1988; Peters, 1991). This tendency for long-term financial assets to deviate from the normal curve is illustrated in Figure 2.4. While there are very few observations in a normal distribution above or below two or three

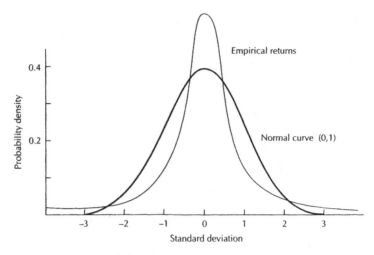

Figure 2.4 Normal distribution and financial asset returns. (Normal distribution from Hastings, 1975.)

standard deviations from the mean, actual long-term financial returns may include observations as much as six standard deviations away, as found by Turner and Weigel and by Peters in stock returns from 1928 to 1988. On the other hand, long-term empirical stock returns show more data points in the center of the distribution than the assumption of normality predicts; these indicate greater *peakedness.*

Nelson (1988) demonstrated the wide variations possible in year-to-year wheat futures price change from 1967 to 1987. These data also show the empirical distribution has a greater central tendency and longer tails than the standard normal curve (Figure 2.5).

Research on stock and asset price change has consistently found that the standard normal distribution does not fit actual events smoothly and Cootner (1964) suggested stock prices may be only approximate standard normal. The normal curve is specifically defined by different measures, or *moments.* The first and second moments are the mean and standard deviation. The third moment of the normal distribution is *skewness* or *tilt;* in these cases the mode is not the same as the mean, and the mode may be either skewed to the left or right. Skewness or tilt is evident in long-term financial asset price change.

The fourth moment of the normal distribution is *kurtosis,* or the degree of thickness in the tails and peakedness of the center; a thick-tailed distribution shows *platykurtosis* while a more peaked

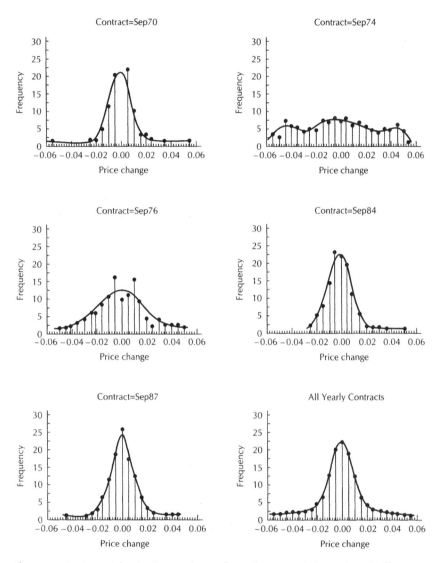

Figure 2.5 Logarithmic September wheat futures. (Selected and all years, 1967–1987, from Nelson, 1988.)

distribution shows *leptokurtosis*. Most studies of long-term stock and asset returns show that price changes have both leptokurtic (peakedness) and platykurtic (thick-tailed) features but that neither theoretical curve alone fits the empirical data.

When differences between the actual returns and a standard normal curve are calculated, an error curve is derived. Peters (1991) computed this error curve for actual stock returns from

1928 to 1988 as shown in Figure 2.6. The normal curve was compared with the frequencies of occurrence for Standard & Poor's 500 five-day returns.

Another reason why the assumption of log normality for asset price change has been questioned is that these models cannot easily handle American options, which have the possibility of early exercise. Additionally, log-normal models become increasingly inaccurate as the term of the option lengthens, especially longer than a year (Wong, 1991).

All fair-value models accept the theoretical link between asset price change and probability theory, but some have abandoned the normality assumption and proposed alternative price change models based on different probability assumptions. Alternative explanations of price change seek, in effect, to eliminate the error curve formed as the difference between the normal and the asset price change.

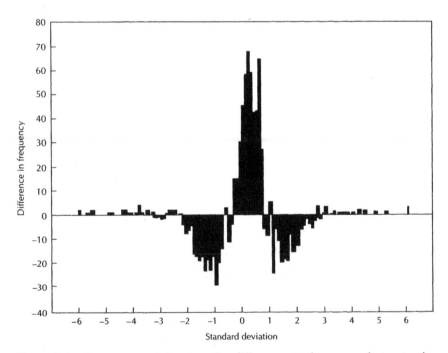

Figure 2.6 Error curve derived as the difference in frequency between the Standard & Poor's 500 five-day returns (1928–1988) and a normal curve. (Copyright ©1991 Edgar Peters. Reprinted by permission of John Wiley & Sons, Inc.)

Mandlebrot (1964) suggested that stock returns may resemble a class of Paretian distributions also known as fractals, which have unstable variance. Peters (1991) shows, however, that a wide range of recent financial asset price changes fit fractal assumptions and models.

The Cauchy distribution (Figure 2.7) has a density function with longer tails than the normal distribution and also tends toward peakedness. Indeed, the Cauchy seems to provide a better fit of long-term wheat futures change than a normal distribution. Unfortunately, the Cauchy has an unstable mean and infinite variance, which complicate its statistical use. Nevertheless, the Cauchy has been used effectively in a number of scientific fields (see Olkin, Gleser, and Derman, 1980).

Recently, fair-value models based on the probability of binomial walks have been proposed, following the work of William Sharpe (1978) who derived the same result as Black and Scholes using only elementary mathematics. These binomial models, also known as lattice-based models, are an exciting area of option research at present. Cox and Rubenstein (1985), who have developed binomial models, also suggest that asset changes may follow some sort of *diffusion-jump* process. Gastineau (1988) has proposed models based on nonnormal distributions of change in option and asset pricing. For European options, binomial models will converge with the BSM model at the limit, but binomial models appear better able to incorporate American option features (Wong, 1991).

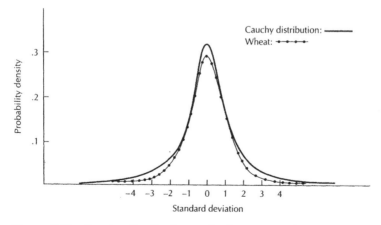

Figure 2.7 Cauchy distribution and wheat price change (1967–1987). (*Source of wheat data:* R. D. Nelson, 1988.)

Both the log-normal and the lattice option models depend upon what one assumes short-term interest rates will be over a long time for back-month options. For this reason, these models are somewhat insensitive to the true *costs of carry* of the underlying asset, which are very important for option prices. An accurate option pricing model, therefore, seeks to take into account both short- and long-term rates of interest, or the term structure. Recently, a number of innovative term-structure binomial models have been put forward for bond options and bond option, traders may wish to study these models more closely (Wong, 1991).

All option traders should be familiar with the statistical assumptions of the model they are using and feel comfortable with them. Most option traders and market makers, however, are traders, not statisticians. To aid the understanding of basic concepts, this book will continue to use the BSM model for illustration, but some modifications of this model will be introduced in later chapters so as to fit prevailing market conditions better.

Fortunately, the BSM model may often be used by option market makers for practical trading to produce reliable results since making option markets is more a question of relative pricing than absolute pricing. Market makers are not so much interested in what real or true fair value may be as in which options are mispriced relative to each other under the same model.

Moreover, one can introduce sophisticated modifications to the BSM model, if needed, by incorporating a strike skew function, which will be discussed elsewhere. For these reasons, the BSM model is used as the statistical basis of this study, and the model will be considered *robust* to the violation of the assumptions of normality. A partial list of software that may be used for calculating option fair values from the BSM model is included in the Appendix.

VOLATILITY

The standard normal fair-value models, such as the BSM model, depend upon five independent variables or unknowns for non–income-earning asset options: interest rates, asset price, strike, expiration date, and standard deviation. Volatility in the BSM model is just the standard deviation of asset prices around the mean over a one-year period. If an underlying asset has a 10% volatility and current price of 100, then there would be a 68% chance (assuming

a normal distribution of price changes) that the asset price at the
end of the year would be within the range of 90 to 110.

The general formula for the standard deviation is:

$$SD = \sqrt{\frac{\Sigma(P - \overline{P})^2}{N}}$$

where   SD = standard deviation

P = price

$\overline{P}$ = mean price

N = number of trials

Here is an example:

(P)rice	$(P - \overline{P})^2$
90	100
100	
110	100
Mean = 100	Σ = 200

The standard deviation, then, would be $\sqrt{200/3}$ = 8.16. In this
example, one standard deviation is 8.16 above or below the mean
of 100. The probability of an event being within one standard deviation on one side of the mean is about 34 percent, or within one
standard deviation above or below the mean is about 68 percent.
In this example, the final price over one year will be within 91.84
and 108.16 about 68 percent of the time.

To avoid the possibility of negative asset prices, standard deviation is customarily calculated using natural logs of rates of change
in lieu of absolute difference. In this case, the formula for the standard deviation is expressed as a rate of change.

$$SDV = \sqrt{\frac{\Sigma(\ln R - \overline{R})^2}{N - 1}}$$

where $R = \dfrac{P_{(t+1)}}{P_{(t)}}$

Computation of the SDV gives a percentage change of the standard deviation and is what is meant by volatility. This volatility is always historical, since it depends for its data upon actual past market fluctuations. SDV may also be called historical volatility (HV). Historical volatility may be used to derive the standard deviation in absolute points (SDP) through the general formula:

$$\text{SDP} = P \times \text{HV}$$

For example, if historical volatility is 0.10 and the current price is 100, then SDP will be 10 points over one year. Knowing how to compute the standard deviation in points is useful to know, as will be evident in later chapters.

To adjust for shorter time intervals than one year, volatility must be divided by a time factor. This factor is the square root of the number of periods in a year ($\sqrt{PY}$). For example, the weekly time factor is composed of 52 periods, and $\sqrt{52} = 7.21$. Common time factor adjustments (PY) are:

Daily	$\sqrt{250}$ =	15.81
	$\sqrt{365}$ =	19.10
Weekly	$\sqrt{52}$ =	7.21
Monthly	$\sqrt{12}$ =	3.46
Bimonthly	$\sqrt{6}$ =	2.45
Quarterly	$\sqrt{4}$ =	2.00

The BSM model calls for the use of calendar days (365), not trading days (250) to expiration, as a time adjustment, but market practitioners often use the number of trading days as the adjustment factor. Is it reasonable to assume that all calendar days are equal for calculating price change, or is the number of trading days a better adjustment divisor?

The answer to this question is a straightforward empirical matter. If the futures price change between Friday's close and Monday's close is equal to or greater than the price change within an average consecutive three-day trading period, then calendar days carry implicit trading volatility risk that should be taken into account. If the weekend price change is equal to or less than an intraweek daily price change, then there would appear to be no weekend volatility effect, and thus the time between Friday's close and Monday's open could be treated as a one-day change, justifying

the use of a 250-day yearly period. In either case, the answer is
easily settled empirically for any specific market.

In summary the formula to find the standard deviation in
points (SDP$_t$) over period PY is:

$$SDP_t = P\left(\frac{V}{\sqrt{PY}}\right)$$

For example, if V is 15 percent and P is 100, then the standard
deviation over one day is 0.95 points, using 250 calendar days.

$$0.95 = 100\left(\frac{.15}{15.81}\right)$$

If one knows the point standard deviation change over a year
and wishes to calculate volatility, the above formula is solved in
this manner:

$$V = \frac{SDP}{P}$$

Thus, a 1.25-point SD over a year for a commodity priced at 100
indicates that volatility is 0.0125, or 1.25 percent.

To find the volatility (V_t) over any period PY:

$$V_t = \frac{SDP_t}{P}\sqrt{PY}$$

$$V_t(\text{in percent}) = V_t \times 100$$

This relationship is sometimes also known as the $T^{1/2}$ Rule; variance is equal to the standard deviation times the square root of
time. For example, the historical volatility over one day is 0.382
(or 38.2%) if SDP daily standard deviation is 2.00 and P is 100:

$$.382 = \frac{2}{100} \times 19.1$$

Given the importance of volatility in option pricing models,
alternative measures of expressing volatility have been variously
proposed. Instead of using only price change from daily close to
close, it is possible to use a volatility measure based on daily
high and low prices. Conceptually this measure makes sense since
differences in day-to-day price closes may be flat even though large

price volatility occur intraday. If the underlying asset is regularly traded in a liquid market, the high/low estimate of volatility may be more accurate than the close/close volatility estimate for identical time periods (Bookstaber, 1987).

In particular, a price change measure of volatility may not work well with bond options, since bond prices converge to par at maturity. For debt markets, yield change has been found to be a better measure of standard deviation in bond option models (Wong, 1991). Finally, one must remember that these volatility and standard deviation measures will only work as long as actual price change can be described by a normal curve.

Standard deviation, or volatility, is perhaps the most important variable in the BSM model. While four of the five variables in the BSM model all are easily known at any one time (futures price, strike, expiration, and interest rates), volatility is not. Thus, even if the distribution of futures price changes tends to resemble a lognormal curve over time, it is still necessary to know the width of the curve (that is, its standard deviation) before one can calculate an option's fair value. But here a problem arises: What measure of volatility is to be used?

When discussing price volatility one must distinguish among three different aspects of volatility: future, historical, and implied. Future volatility is the standard deviation that would be calculated from the present to some period in the future. In a sense, this is the real volatility. For the BSM formula to work as theoretically intended, the measure of standard deviation that one must use is the future (or real) volatility. Obviously, what is of interest is not what has happened, but what will happen.

However, since the future is unknowable, so is future volatility. Since the fair-value model cannot work without knowledge of future volatility some estimate must be made in order to use the BSM formula. There are two ways of estimating what future volatility may be: use either historical or implied levels of volatility.

Historical volatility is the empirical standard deviation of futures prices from some time in the past up to the present. Since it has already happened, historical volatility is always known with certainty. The only judgment to be exercised concerning historical volatility is the period to be selected. Half-year, 90-day, 20-day, and even 10-day periods have been used. However, each of these different periods is likely to provide a different estimate of volatility level, and indeed there may be no single best estimate of historical volatility. Generally, long-period estimates are the most stable and

shorter periods the most unstable and erratic because the latter
are subject to immediate market conditions.

The use of historical volatility in the BSM model (for whatever
period chosen) would not present a problem for option fair-value
determinations if future volatility levels happened to coincide with
past volatility levels. If what has happened will always happen,
then future volatility can be estimated directly from historical levels confidently.

Unfortunately, not only is there no a priori reason for past
and future volatility to be the same, but also the record shows
they usually are not, whatever period is used. Future volatility
often changes over time, rendering historical volatility a poor and
unreliable estimator of future volatility, whatever the period of
historical volatility used.

In statistical terms the difference between past and future
volatility is known as *heteroscedasticity,* or the variance of the
variance over time. This difference represents a problem to the
uncritical use of estimators based on the assumption of statistical
normality in any time series model. The existence of severe heteroscedasticity over commodity cycles is intuitively well known;
commodity prices are sometimes quiet for extended periods, and
then break out in extreme price runs in one direction or another,
before returning to quiescence again. Historical volatility is a poor
predictor of future volatility.

Implied option volatility may be used as an alternative to historical volatility in estimating future volatility. Whenever an option is traded at market price, it is possible to work backward in
the BSM formula and solve for volatility. The resultant *implied*
volatility is the market's current estimate of future volatility, and
is an alternative to using historical volatility as a forecaster of
future volatility.

There is little evidence, however, that current implied levels of
volatility are reliable or accurate estimates of future volatility To
see this intuitively, suppose that "real" future volatility will be indicated in the 20-day historical volatility lagged backward 20 days.
Current 20-day historical volatility, for example, is only the future
volatility 20 days ago. When historical volatility is lagged and then
compared with the level of implied volatility at that time, there
is little indication that implied levels will necessarily equal real
volatility. Sometimes implied levels fall below real future volatility and sometimes they are above, as illustrated for October cotton
futures and options in Figure 2.8.

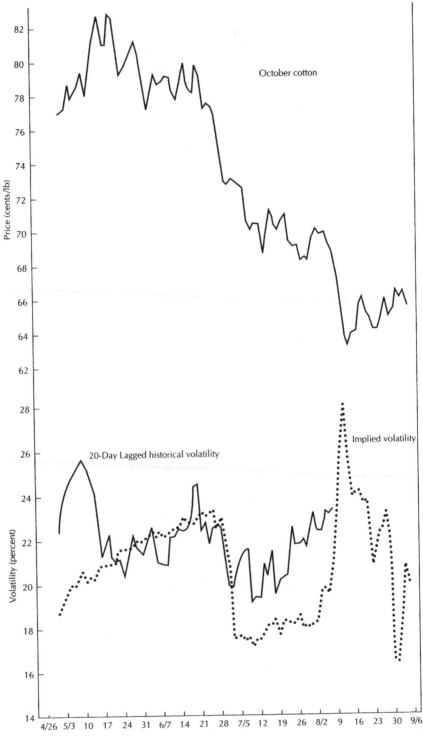

Figure 2.8 Real and implied volatility for October cotton futures and option prices. (*Source:* Mr. Tom Bertolini, New York Cotton Exchange.)

Generally, there is no consistent short-term pattern between real future volatility and implied levels in most option markets. Since real or future volatility may never be known until after the fact, one must estimate future volatility from either unlagged historical volatility or current implied volatilities in the market in order to derive accurate fair-value option prices. If neither is a reliable empirical predictor of future volatility, then the robustness of the BSM option pricing model is weakened.

For the most part, this uncertainty is not a serious impediment for market makers to using the BSM model. Prudently profitable market making does not depend, for the most part, on knowledge of true future volatility and, therefore, true fair-value prices, but rather on relative pricing. In practice, market makers almost always initially set bid/asked prices around recent implied volatility levels, and only use historical levels for reference.

FINANCIAL AND FUTURES OPTIONS

The discussion of options thus far has been generally restricted to options on non–income-earning spot instruments, or to all options in general. Nevertheless, options will display different characteristics depending upon the differences of the underlying asset: stocks, stock indexes, bonds, currency, commodities, or futures on these. One important distinction among option markets is the cost of carry for the underlying asset, whether positive or negative.

For most financial assets (stocks, bonds, and currency) there is an initial positive cost of carry, with income from dividends, yield, or interest. In the case of stock dividends, for example, where the dividend will reduce the price of the stock by that amount, the current price of the stock must be discounted by this dividend amount when considering the value of the in-the-money or intrinsic option at expiration. For example, if a stock priced at 100 is paying a $1 dividend quarterly, then the 90 day option with strike of 100 will be on a stock worth only $99 after dividend payout, assuming no further price changes by expiration. What is of importance for the option is not necessarily the current stock price but the present estimate of expected future value. In this example this estimate would be $99 and, in effect, the forward price.

For some assets, such as commodities like gold or copper, there is a negative cost of carry due to costs of storage, insurance, shipment, and so on for physical assets. This negative cost of carry will tend to raise the forward price. In the bond market in particular, where bonds are often financed by other bonds, both positive and negative cost-of-carry positions are possible. For example, if a holding in long-term U.S. Treasury bonds is being financed by a sale of short-term Treasury bills, there will be a positive cost of carry if bill rates are below long rates, but a negative carry if short rates exceed long rates. In summary, differences between income- or yield-producing assets (stocks, bonds, currency) and non–income- or negative-earning assets require that option models be adjusted for asset price cost of carry.

Options on real underlying assets and options on futures also need to be distinguished. For example, an option on stocks or stock indexes is a call or put right that corresponds to an ongoing similar underlying asset. In this sense, a January call is a right on the same stock asset as a May call. However, futures options are rights to futures contracts and not to the underlying asset itself. A January futures call holds a right against a different underlying asset (the January futures contract) than a May call (the May futures contract). Since futures options introduce new complexities into option market making, let us briefly review futures markets here.

A futures contract is the right to take delivery of a specified quantity and quality of a commodity (spot) at the monthly expiration specified in the contract. Thus, if a trader is long (bought) a December sugar futures, at a specific day in September, the trader can take delivery of 112,000 pounds of a specified grade of sugar at a certified warehouse. If a trader is short (sold) a similar futures contract, then he or she must stand ready to deliver spot at expiration. A futures contract of itself does not specify any price at which delivery is to take place. Rather, the purchase (or sale) cost of the contract, when first purchased or sold on the market, becomes the basis cost to buyer or seller. In modern futures markets, contract expiration and delivery dates are sequenced in cycles every quarter or several months apart.

In economic theory, futures markets are useful because they allow for efficient price discovery and for investment risk shifting, or price insurance. Futures markets provide an efficient and competitive price-setting mechanism ("discovery") by allowing prices to respond immediately to shifting supply-and-demand conditions through an ongoing open outcry auction market. Futures markets also provide a risk-shifting function to producers, merchants, and industrial consumers, allowing industry to shift future price-change risk to other commercial interests, dealers, or speculators. This risk shifting allows business to achieve neutralization of risk and thereby improve trade efficiency.

For example, a farmer will typically sell forward to a merchant all or part of his or her crop that has not yet been harvested. This sale protects, or hedges, the price of the crop while it is still being grown. This action helps avoid the price pressures associated with seasonal harvesting and temporary oversupply. Mining or petroleum producers also use futures contracts in this way, to hedge against oversupplies.

Likewise, a merchant will sell forward if shipping to the destination market requires a long time, exposing the commodity to unexpected price shifts before sale. In the early days of forward trading, a merchant would buy cotton in Savannah and then ship it north to New York, before reshipping it to New England or Liverpool textile mills. By selling forward, the merchant protected his investment in inventory during the long lag between purchase and final delivery. Hedging crude oil during its long transport to market is a more recent example.

Also, manufacturers who use commodity raw products will typically hedge their cost of inventory during production by either selling or buying forward. Cotton mills today, much like the nineteenth century, still have routine recourse to forward contracts in controlling inventory costs.

Futures markets in the nineteenth century and on into the twentieth century were dominated by trading in agricultural products and precious or industrial metals; these remain a significant proportion of all modern futures trading. In the last several decades, however, currency, bond, and stock index futures have been traded, and they now account for the largest proportion of all futures trading. Worldwide, the growth of futures trading has been explosive as the financial industry learned that futures trading may be used to manage and hedge portfolios of bonds, stocks, or currencies.

Futures need not and usually do not trade at the same price as the underlying spot commodity; the difference in price is referred to as the *basis*. If the underlying commodity is a non–income-earning asset that must be stored somewhere, the futures price is usually higher than the spot commodity price in order to account for the cost of storage or negative carry. For non-income stored negative carry markets, futures prices will trade over spot (positive basis), and the more distant futures will trade over near futures prices, to account for the requisite costs of storage and insurance. When the distant futures price exceeds the near futures price, the market is said to be in *contango*.

If the near futures price is higher than the distant price, however, the market is said to be backward (Figure 2.9). *Backwardation* in the futures time spread for non–income-earning durable commodities may come about for several reasons. In agricultural commodities there is often a normal backwardation between crop year futures cycles, which comes about because the storage costs of the new crop are unrelated to storage costs of the old or current crop. If the new crop has not yet been harvested, no storage costs have been incurred; and the far distant futures contract may trade, therefore, lower than the less distant or near contracts. Also, in both seasonal and nonseasonal commodity markets, backwardation may occur as a result of severe supply shortages or sharp increases in unfilled demand. For example, although gold and silver futures normally trade in contango, during the 1980–81 attempted silver corner by Bunker Hunt, precious metals futures went backward.

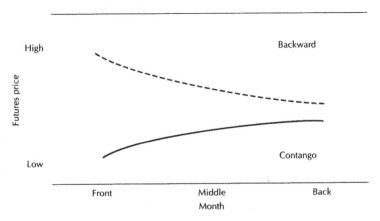

Figure 2.9   Futures contango and backwardation.

For income-earning assets—stocks, bonds, or currency—the futures time spread may be somewhat different from that of non–income-earning assets. For financial assets, the cost of carry is not negative, and may even be positive. Stocks and bonds earn dividends or interest, and do not entail large costs of storage. For assets with a positive cost of carry the futures time spread is normally backward. In effect, the future price is discounted by the positive yield on the asset over time, and thus distant futures prices may trade lower than near-term prices, all else equal. Consider, for example, the situation in which one-year Treasury notes, par 100, yield 5 percent over one year. If one year forward futures contracts are priced at 95, they would approximately discount the positive cost of carry and trade at normal backwardation. Positive carry futures markets, however, also may display contango time spreads at times, for different reasons. Further discussion on time and basis spreads of futures may be found in works listed in the bibliography (Williams, 1986).

Futures options have rights over a futures contract, not the underlying asset. This distinction introduces important new risks to option traders, who make markets in futures options time spreads. The risk does not exist for stock option traders, however. It is also possible to have option markets on both the underlying asset and the futures on the underlying asset. For example, there are options markets on stock indexes at the same time that options on the futures of the stock index are being traded in a different market. This situation opens up the possibility of intermarket option arbitrage. This study will emphasize futures options as the general case, with discussion of differences arising with stock or bond options where appropriate.

3

Option Risks

INTRODUCTION TO OPTION RISKS

Fair-value option models link statistical theory to investment risk, which modern capital theory defines as the probability that the actual return from an investment will differ from the expected return (Hagin, 1979; Gehm, 1983). Defined this way, investment risk is useful in evaluating portfolios that have equal profit but differ in risk taken. The chances of doubling one's money on a single toss of the dice in a casino promises a better rate of return than the interest earned in a bank account, but runs radically different risks. Capital may seek the largest profit, but at the "best" risk/reward ratio.

The link between probability theory and investment risk makes it possible to quantify option investment risk in very precise ways. Except for strike, any change in the other variables in the fair-value option model (interest rate, futures price change, days to expiration, and volatility) may bring about changes in option prices over the duration of the option cycle until expiration. Thus, these variables represent *risks* to an option portfolio.

This chapter briefly characterizes each fundamental risk to an option's price. These risks are defined as delta (Δ, futures price change), gamma (Γ, change in delta), theta (Θ, time decay change), kappa (K)/vega (implied volatility change), and rho (P, interest rate change). Vertical spreads across single calendar strikes also are subject to a *skew risk* in the implied volatility strike spread. Holding calendar or time spreads exposes option positions to additional risks: time delta (spread futures price change) and time kappa/vega (spread option implied volatility change). In addition to these market-based risks, there are also extramarket financial risks.

For the purpose of illustration risk to an option will generally be quoted in dollar-and-cent amounts for a single hypothetical option in this text. However, the real dollar risk must be multiplied by the value of the actual option contract, which will vary depending upon the type of option. For example, a 10-cent gamma risk may not seem large when one is considering only one option, but this 10 cents must be multiplied by the dollar value of the actual option on the asset or futures contract. For example, if the futures option or asset moves $500 for every whole futures point, a 10-cent risk is really a $50 risk for one option ($0.10 × $500), and a 10-option position would have a $500 gamma risk. Likewise, a single stock option represents an option on 100 shares of stock and a 10-cent risk on a stock option is really a risk of $10.00.

In trading options it is easy to lose your shirt if you do not understand the variety of risks involved. These risks will be illustrated in the following sections using simple option positions.

DELTA (Δ) RISK

The delta risk of an option is a ratio reflecting the dollar amount of change in an option price for every dollar change in the underlying futures price. The delta risk is also known as the *hedge ratio*.

$$\Delta = \frac{\text{Dollar change in option price}}{\text{Positive dollar change in asset price}}$$

When an option's value increases with a positive change in asset price, delta is positive. If an option's delta is +.30, for example, the option will increase in value 30 cents for every positive dollar change in asset price. If an option's delta is −.30, then it will decrease in value 30 cents for every positive dollar change in asset price.

Figure 3.1 shows the payoff of a long 100 strike call and its delta over a range of futures prices from 90 to 110 at 60 days, 30 days, and one day to (or at) expiration (with implied volatility levels at 15 and interest at 10 percent).

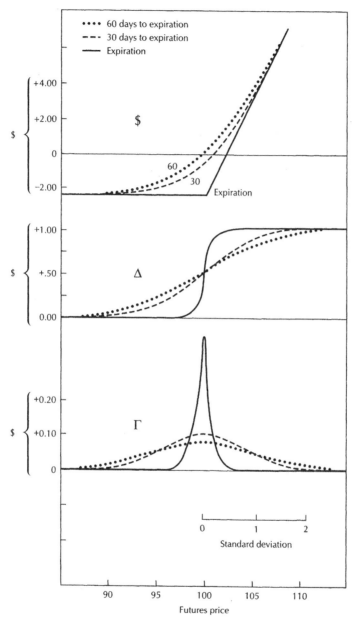

Figure 3.1 Delta and gamma risks of a long 100 strike call and its payoff.

When futures or the asset itself are at the strike of the call, the delta of the long call always is a +.50. It can range upward to +1.00 when futures are above the strike and to zero when futures are below the strike. A short call would have a negative delta, since it would be the inverse or opposite side of the long call. The long put has a negative delta and the short put a positive delta. The delta of these and other option positions are discussed in more detail in Chapter 4.

A very deep in-the-money option will usually have a delta close to 1.00, that is, the option price will move almost exactly as the asset price itself. This correspondence makes intuitive sense, since a deep in-the-money option is likely to expire with the value of the underlying asset and, therefore, will move in value almost equally. Likewise, a very far out-of-the-money option usually has a very small delta, which is asymptotically approaching zero. This pattern also makes intuitive sense, since a far out-of-the-money option is likely to be worthless at expiration and to be relatively unresponsive to underlying asset price changes.

An at-the-money option will always move in price about half that of an asset contract, for a delta of $\pm$.50, reflecting the equal probability of an option expiring in or out of the money. Generally, no single option can have a delta greater than +1.00 or less than −1.00 since no single option can change, dollar for dollar, more than a single asset contract at expiration. The underlying asset itself will always have a delta of +1.00 or −1.00, depending upon whether a long or short position is held.

The passage of time increases or decreases the delta of an option. An in-the-money option will show an increasing delta and an out-of-the-money option a decreasing delta. Option delta, therefore, *drifts* in time. This delta drift becomes more pronounced as the option expiration approaches reflecting the time shrinkage of the standard deviation, all else being equal.

In statistical terms, an option's delta is also the probability that at expiration the futures will settle above the option strike, making the option in-the-money. A delta risk is a futures or asset price-based risk. A high positive delta indicates that in-the-money options are likely to remain in-the-money, and a low positive delta indicates the likelihood that the option will expire worthless. At-the-money options with a delta of +.50, therefore, have a 50:50 chance of expiring in- or out-of-the-money.

A positive delta indicates a bullish option position and a negative delta reflects a bearish one. A long call or short put is a positive delta position, and a short call or long put is a negative delta, for example. The delta of a total option position is simply the net sum of the delta's of all separate positions.

Some option traders and market makers, however, often prefer to remain neutral about market direction, that is, *delta neutral*. To create a delta neutral option position, a trader must offset the deltas of the separate options. For example, if the delta of an at-the-money option is always +.50, then an option position that is long $2 at-the-money calls, and short $1 future, will be delta neutral, that is, $2 \times .50 - 1.00 = 0$. A long or short straddle can also be a delta neutral position if the strike of the straddle is at the current futures price, for example, $(+.50) + (-.50) = 0$. The Δ's of many single-month option strategies will be found in Chapter 4.

GAMMA (Γ) AND LAMBDA (Λ) RISK

An option's delta is not a constant, but changes as the asset price changes and makes the option more or less in-, at-, or out-of-the-money. The change in an option's delta as the asset price moves up or down is referred to as gamma risk.

$$\Gamma = \frac{\text{Net change in } \Delta}{\text{Dollar change in asset price}}$$

While delta is a measure of risk to price from asset price change, gamma is a measure of the risk due to the stability of the delta. As the asset price increases $1.00, the delta of an out-of-the-money long call will increase, for example, from .30 to .35. This .05-cent increase in the delta is the gamma of the call position at that futures price range, and represents the added risk to an option when delta changes.

Gamma can be negative as well as positive. A long call or long put always has a positive gamma, and a short call or short put always has a negative gamma throughout the entire futures price range, with a single modal peak centering around at-the-money options. The deep in- or out-of-the-money wing options have the least change in delta and, therefore, the lowest gamma (Figure 3.1).

For example, at 60 days to expiration, the long 100 call still has some positive probability of expiring in-the-money and, therefore, will have a positive delta and a positive gamma over the range of futures prices from 90 to 110. When futures are at strike (100), gamma is 0.075 cents at 60 days to expiration; gamma rises to 0.10 cents at 30 days, but with a smaller range.

By one day to expiration, however, the same option that was once very deep out-of-the money has virtually no chance of expiring in-the-money, and its delta and gamma have shrunk to zero. By one day to expiration, the gamma of the long 100 call will have exploded to over 0.25 cents when futures are at strike, but very deep in-the-money options will have a high positive delta but gamma at zero since delta has reached its upward limit of one. Generally, at-the-money options show an increase in gamma as expiration approaches, while the deep in-the-money or out-of-the-money option gamma decreases over time. The gamma risk of many single-month option positions is found in Chapter 4.

Another measure closely related to delta is the *elasticity*, or lambda, of an option position; lambda is defined as the percent change in the value of an option position relative to the percent change in the value of the underlying asset.

$$\Lambda = \frac{\text{Percent change in option value}}{\text{Percent change in asset price}}$$

The lambda of an option will always be greater than one, since an option is a leveraged instrument relative to the underlying asset. A deep in-the-money option with little time remaining to expiration will have a lambda approaching one, reflecting equal proportional changes between option and asset. As an option becomes out-of-the-money, its lambda will become much greater than one, indicating its higher leveraged power for gain or loss relative to the underlying security.

THETA (Θ) RISK

The change in option price due to the days remaining to expiration is known as time decay, or theta risk.

$$\Theta = \frac{\text{Change in option's value}}{\text{One-day change in time remaining to expiration}}$$

This risk should be obvious since, all else being equal, an option contract with fewer days remaining is worth less than an equivalent one with more days to expiration, for the extra days add value. Thus, option prices tend to decline as expiration approaches, and indeed, decline more rapidly the closer the expiration is.

For example, the theta risk of a short 100 call at 60 days to expiration is only +2.5 cents per day when futures remain at the strike price, which means that the trader will profit by this amount for one day by time decay. At 30 days, the short call will have a theta just under +4 cents, which will rise to over +10 cents on the last day before expiration so long as futures remain at a strike of 100. If there is a move in either direction, however, the in- or out-of-the-money option will have a smaller theta risk (Figure 3.2).

If an option trader is long an option, each day brings some decrease in the option's value, all else being equal, and the trader is exposed to negative theta. Short options will have a positive theta, for the short option seller will profit from the time decay value of an option. To be *short premium* is to have a positive theta, because the trader expects to make a profit from time value decay. Generally, at-the-money options with the least amount of time remaining to expiration will experience the largest positive or negative theta values. The time value decay is slowest with long trading life remaining in the option.

Note that the theta of a long call is strikingly similar in form to its gamma risk over this range of asset prices, except that theta is about half the magnitude of gamma and of opposite sign. The identity of risk between gamma and theta in single-month options will be important in the evaluation of risk in the more complex option positions and strategies that are discussed in later chapters.

KAPPA (K)/VEGA RISK

Even if there is no change in futures or asset price risk (delta or gamma) or in time risk (theta), an option price may be affected by changes in the market's valuation of implied volatility. This valuation is formally referred to as kappa, although popular usage also refers to this risk as *vega*. Kappa /vega risk is one of the most important risks to an option price and is defined in this manner:

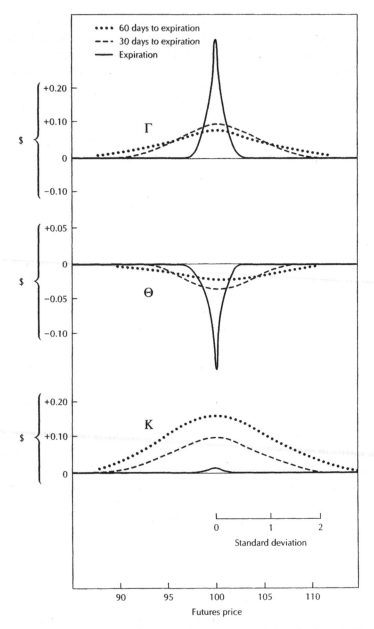

Figure 3.2 Gamma, theta, and kappa/vega risks of a long 100 call.

$$K/\text{vega} = \frac{\text{Dollar change in option price}}{\text{Positive one-point implied volatility change}}$$

For example, an increase in the implied volatility from 15 to 16 (one point) would increase the value of a long 100 strike call by a positive 16 cents at 60 days to expiration when futures are trading at the strike price (Figure 3.2). The kappa/vega of the long call would be positive over all futures price ranges but would move either upward or downward as the call became in or out of the money. Of course, there is no limit on the increase in implied volatility. Were a 10-point increase in implied levels to happen, the long (short) call would have a profit (loss) of $1.60.

This amount must be multiplied by the actual value of the option contract to determine the precise dollar risk. For a single stock option on 100 shares of stock, the amounts above must be multiplied by 100; and for a futures option that has a value of $500 per contract point, the above kappa/vega amounts would be multiplied by that full point value. Thus, a $1.60 kappa/vega risk in the above example would represent an $800 risk to the holder of one futures option and $8000 to the holder of 10!

An option position will have a positive, negative, or neutral kappa/vega risk at any single asset or futures price. Positive kappa/vega risk will result in increased profits from increased implied volatility, and negative kappa/vega will result in a loss from increased implied volatility change. A long call is positive kappa/vega and a short call, negative. A long put is also positive kappa/vega and a short put, negative. To be *long volatility* means that a trader has a positive kappa/vega option position.

Remember, kappa/vega risk does not vary directly with delta risk; they must be treated separately. Implied volatilities of options may move independent of futures price changes in either price direction. For purposes of illustration, let us suppose an important announcement (such as weekly USDA export sales) is scheduled for the following day; the price directional implications of this announcement are unknown. Option prices might rise on an increased market estimate of the possible future price change after the announcement, and might fall just as rapidly after the announcement if futures price change did not occur, all else being equal. The increase and decrease in option prices before and after this announcement reflect changes in the market's implied volatility price.

Paradoxically, sudden sharp futures price changes (up or down) may occur in conjunction with falling implied volatilities. This divergence might seem counterintuitive, since if real volatility is up, one might suppose that implied volatility must be up also. However, one would be ignoring that implied volatility is the market's estimate of future volatility, not historical volatility. An increase in current volatility accompanied by a fall in implied volatility merely suggests that the market expects future volatility to fall, however high it currently is.

It is not uncommon for option traders to be long a call and find, when futures prices do move sharply higher, that their call has increased only marginally in price even with a moderate positive delta. While such traders are likely to be upset and perhaps even blame the market maker for somehow cheating them out of their profit, what the option traders do not realize is that the price paid for the call had already been based on a high-volatility estimate. Once the move had occurred, the market believed no further moves were likely and lowered its estimate of volatility. Although the option traders were correct about price movement, they were whipsawed by the market's changing estimate of volatility. These traders did not understand kappa /vega risk (see letters to *Barron's*, April 18, and July 18, 1988). One exaggerated example of the possibility for a trader to be correct about the direction of the market but still lose money in options because of an implied volatility change occurred in the stock market crash of October 1987, when short out-of-the-money call options rose in price after the 500-point drop in the market, reflecting a market-implied volatility level of well over 100!

In practice, the implied volatilities of options are one of the major risks to any option trader. Much analysis, evaluation, and strategy are devoted to kappa/vega risk.

RHO (P) RISK

One of the variables in the BSM futures option-pricing model is the risk-free rate of interest. This interest rate represents the cost of carry of an option position, or the opportunity cost to capital of trading in options, that is, what unoccupied capital may safely earn. A positive cost of carry earns interest, and a negative cost of carry incurs interest payments. The appropriate risk-free rate of interest is taken from the yield curve of the U.S. Treasury bill market that matches the option cycle. If interest rates change, the cost of carry and the value of an option will also change, all else being equal. Change in the cost of carry that leads to change in the value of an option is referred to as rho risk.

Consider a futures call which has a hypothetical fair value of $100 and a zero cost of carry, that is, the cost of capital is free. The purchase or sale of the fair-value call at $100 results in neither profit nor loss over the long run. But if capital is not free, the buyer of the $100 call must deposit cash to purchase the option (a negative carry). Thus, he or she forfeits the earned interest on the $100, and the seller gains the use of these funds, which may be deposited to earn interest after having satisfied margin requirements. If the call is to have a fair value that includes the cost of carry, the call will sell at some discount to $100 that equals the cost of interest rate carry.

Therefore, as interest rates increase, the fair value of futures options falls, all else being equal. For example, the fair value of a 100 call with 200 days to expiration, a volatility of 15, and a risk-free rate of interest of 8 percent, is $4.24. If interest rates were to rise from 8 to 15 percent, however, the value of the option would drop to $4.08. The 16-cent difference represents the discount on $4.24 of an additional 8 percent annual interest prorated for 200 days.

For nonfutures options, such as stock options, an increase in interest may either increase or decrease the value of the option. An increase in interest will increase the carrying cost of long stock positions, making a call option more desirable than holding stock. Likewise, an increase in interest will make shorting the stock more attractive than holding a long put, in which case the value of the put will decline.

The impact on option prices of a change in the risk-free rate of interest is not so large as that of some other option price risks. Interest rates rarely move so dramatically over six-month periods as the previous example might imply, although the early 1980s did witness extraordinarily high historical interest rate changes. In some foreign option markets these interest rate changes may also not be unusual.

Interest rates, nevertheless, remain an important market risk and necessitate sophisticated strategies for market makers. These will be discussed in Chapter 5.

SKEW RISK

The central implied volatility of an option strike series is that found in the level of the at-the-money straddle. But if the 100 call is trading at an implied level of 15, what about the 105 call, or any other options of this cycle, whatever the strike?

All strikes of one calendar series need not trade at the at-the-money implied level. A 100 call may be trading at a 15 volatility, but a 105 call at a 20 implied volatility. This difference in the implied volatility levels of single-cycle options across strikes is termed the *implied volatility slope,* or *skew.*

Positive skew refers to both out-of-the-money puts and out-of-the-money calls (wings) that are trading at higher volatility levels than at-the-money options (center). For a flat skew, all strikes trade at approximately the same volatility levels. In a negative skew the option wings trade at lower volatilities than the center strike options. Since puts and calls each have different out-of-the-money/in-the-money volatility spreads, there is a put skew and a call skew in every single-cycle strike series. These hypothetical skew relations are shown in Figure 3.3.

Skew risk exists in any spread option position because the degree of implied skew may change. If a skew goes from positive to flat to negative, vertical spread traders are affected, as changes in skew affect option spread prices. If an implied volatility skew exists, then it generally is a linear or curvilinear function. Sometimes saw-toothed and choppy skews exist temporarily as a result of transient imbalances or trades on close. These are relatively unimportant and may safely be disregarded.

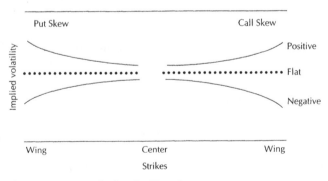

Figure 3.3   Implied volatility skew.

On many if not most futures and financial option markets some form of positive put and call skew exists. In practice, option traders tend to value out-of-the-money options higher than the BSM model suggests. In other words, option market participants trade as if a more frequent or extreme price volatility than log-normal probability suggests is likely. From Chapter 2 we know that actual long-term returns of financial assets have greater extremes than would be expected by the normal distribution, and that these are consistent with implied volatility skew.

Positive skew patterns are also consistent with assumptions of popular option trading strategies. Option speculators may prefer to be long out-of-the-money options, owing to their relatively low absolute cost and low absolute risk of loss as well as their infrequent potential for big payoffs (for example, the lottery ticket play). Conversely, option traders may prefer selling at-the-money options because of the greater absolute time decay (positive theta) profits. These market demand situations may tend to lower the implied volatilities of the center and raise those of the wings.

The only common exceptions to the general pervasiveness of positive skews in futures and financial option markets are the sometimes negative call skew in stock index futures options, and the sometimes negative or flat skew in commodity futures puts. Stock option participants devalue out-of-the-money calls and some commodity option markets devalue out-of-the-money puts with negative skews. The topic of skew risk will be taken up again in Chapter 8.

TIME SPREAD RISK

The discussion of option risks so far has been limited to single-month positions only, either as single options or as some type of vertical spread. *Time spreading* means holding a simultaneous position in more than one calendar month; it is also known as a *horizontal* or *calendar spread*. The option leg that is the closest to expiration is termed the *front month,* and the option leg furthest from expiration is known as the *back month.* An option leg between the front and back months would be the *middle month.* Time spreading neutralizes some of the risks of holding single-month positions. At the same time, calendar spreads are subject to other time-based risks that may be as severe or more severe than those risks neutralized. The two time-based risks for calendar spreads are termed *time* delta and time kappa/vega *risks*.

Time delta risk is defined as the delta risk to any futures option time spread caused by a change in the underlying futures time basis. Time delta risk is only applicable to futures option positions, and not to cash or stock option positions, since the underlying instrument never expires in stock calendar option spreads (that is, the shares of common stock), while futures price time spreads reflect differential prices of monthly contracts. Time delta risk is obvious to any futures option trader, of course, but less obvious sometimes to traders who only trade stock or cash option spreads. Stocks and the cash market do not have a time basis. Futures and futures options do, and this is the source of time delta risk.

All option calendar spreads, whether futures or nonfutures, are subject to time kappa/vega risk as well. A position composed of two different contract months risks having the implied volatility spread of the different months' change. The implied volatility of a time spread is by no means constant, and exposes a time option spread to price risk, sometimes more than the risk neutralized in a single-month strategy.

Both time delta time kappa/vega are extremely important and will be discussed further in Chapter 6.

EXTRAMARKET RISKS

The risks to the value of an option discussed so far are generally known and may be quantitatively measured. There is another class of option risks that are less well known or measurable. They are the extramarket risks that frequently result from financial irregularities or calamities of one sort or another.

A financial risk to all options and futures traders is the possibility that a trader may lose his or her entire capital in a clearinghouse suspension or bankruptcy. Market makers and exchange option traders are required to keep trading funds in an exchange-regulated clearinghouse that guarantees the trades of its members. Although the clearinghouse system protects a trader from the default of any individual trader with whom he or she trades, it does not protect an exchange trader from the default of the clearinghouse itself. Any floor trader takes the risk that another trader at his or her clearinghouse may suffer losses so large that the clearinghouse itself becomes temporarily or permanently insolvent. This risk is real, and over the years there have been several stock or futures clearinghouse failures, such as Volume Investors in 1985, Fossett in 1989, and Stotler in 1990. Others are bound to happen in the future. Fortunately, in these clearinghouse suspensions virtually no floor traders lost account capital, but of course, it is not impossible that this might happen in the future.

An attendant risk in a suspension of a trader's clearinghouse is that the trader will not have the means to trade the carryover position, exposing the trader to market risk. If a trader is inadvertently long or short in the market and unable to adjust his or her position because a clearinghouse suspension has frozen all accounts, the trader may incur steep losses whether or not the clearinghouse eventually remains insolvent.

Some means do exist to lessen extramarket risks. For instance, the general public may be somewhat safer trading through large brokerages; and stock and currency options are guaranteed settlement through the Options Clearing Corporation. Nevertheless, the large over-the-counter market in options, especially bonds and currencies, has no clearinghouse guarantee system. Therefore, traders are exposed to what is known as *counterparty* risk, which exists when the opposite party to a contract defaults without clearinghouse guarantees. In this case, hypothetical profits turn into losses.

Extramarket risks should be considered carefully by prudent option traders, however improbable. Although they are rare and freak, these risks may be devastating to a market maker's or dealer's capital.

4

Position Risk Profiles

BASIC OPTION POSITIONS

To evaluate option position risks comprehensively, one first must have some working classifications of the universe of possible types of option positions. The basic option positions may be considered to be composed of the 22 core positions listed in Table 4.1.

These positions may be defined briefly as follows (see the Appendix to this chapter for some illustrated examples):

Straddle. Long (short) same strike put and call; for example, long the 100 call and the 100 put.

Strangle. Long (short) different strike put and call; for example, long the 110 call and the 90 put.

Vertical spread. Long (short) and short (long) different strike options; for example long the 100 call, short the 110 call. Vertical spreads may be either bull or bear spreads depending on the directional expectation of price.

Fence. Long (short) put/call and short (long) a different strike call/put; for example, long the 100 call, short the 90 put.

Ratio spread. Long (short) one strike option, and short (long) a greater number of other strike options; for example, long one 100 call, short two 110 calls. There are four possible ratio spreads: long call, short call, long put, and short put. A ratio spread is long or short in the direction of the net options held. For instance, a long call ratio spread is short one 100 call, long two 110 calls. Long ratio spreads are also known as *backspreads.*

Table 4.1 Basic option positions

1 Long call

2 Short call

3 Long put

4 Short put

5 Long straddle/strangle

6 Short straddle/strangle

7 Bull spread

8 Bear spread

9 Bull fence

10 Bear fence

11 Ratio spread long calls (call backspread)

12 Ratio spread long puts (put backspread)

13 Ratio spread short calls

14 Ratio spread short puts

15 Long cartwheel

16 Short cartwheel

17 Long wrangle

18 Short wrangle

19 Long butterfly/condor

20 Short butterfly/condor

21 Conversion/reversal/box

22 Time spreads

Note: See Chapter Appendix for payoff and risk profiles of single-month positions.

Cartwheel. Long one ratio spread and short another ratio spread; for example, short one 100 call, long two 110 calls, long one 100 put, short two 90 puts.

Wrangle. Long (short) both the put and call ratio spreads; for instance, short one 100 call, long two 110 calls, and short one 100 put and long two 90 puts.

Butterfly. Long (short) the middle strike options and short (long) an equal number of outer strike options on both sides of the middle; for example, long one 90 call, short two 100 calls, and long one 110 call. A *condor* means selling (buying) the middle strikes as a strangle rather than as a combination of a straddle. A butterfly or condor is always both a *bull* and *bear spread* combined.

Synthetics. A conversion, reversal or box. Synthetics are generally risk-free option positions composed of some combination of underlying instrument and same-strike puts and calls. These terms are defined and discussed in Chapter 5.

Time Spreads. A time spread is an option position composed of two or more different option calendar cycles (the "legs"). For further details see Chapter 6.

For a simpler classification, this text groups straddles and strangles as one position type, and butterflies and condors as another single type. Straddles/strangles and butterflies/condors are grouped together because members of each pair are essentially similar to each other except for the distance of the strike spread. This study considers the standard vertical ratio spreads as separate positions, and examines several position types less frequently discussed: fences, cartwheels, and wrangles. Conversions, reversals, and boxes may be treated as one position type from the standpoint of risk and are, therefore, one synthetic type.

All time spreads are considered as belonging to one category in Table 4.1. Actually, any time spread may be created in any of the other basic position types, as either a two-legged or three-legged (butterfly) time spread. When time spreads are considered, the number of basic possible positions increases by a factor of 21 for each leg added, since this is the number of the basic single-month positions possible. Because of the complex possibilities of time spreads, this topic will be taken up separately in Chapter 6. This chapter will only discuss single-month option position risks.

There are other option positions, not listed in Table 4.1, that are irregular in one way or another. Irregular option positions are usually some combination of one of the basic option positions, executed separately over a very wide strike/futures range. For example, the payoff schedule of an irregular option position might look like Figure 4.1.

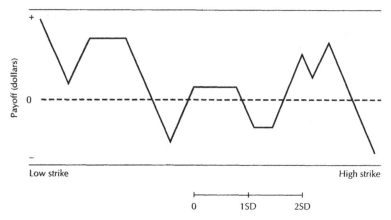

Figure 4.1 Irregular option position expiration payoff.

Irregular option positions are *quirky* and display unstable risk profiles over extremely wide strike or futures price ranges. Essentially any irregular position may be built up with some combination of the 20 basic single-month positions spread across wide strike ranges. *Quirkiness* results from a tendency for a spread to take on the risk characteristics of the nearest strike option to futures near expiration as the absolute standard deviation shrinks as expiration nears. For example, a butterfly position in the back month may take on the risk characteristics of a straddle in the front month as the standard deviation shrinks over time. Almost any extremely large option position that is composed of almost all the strikes traded will have some quirky characteristics very near to expiration. This topic will be reserved until expiration risks are discussed in Chapters 5 and 7.

Dealer positions are rarely composed of only single options or simple spreads. In practice, a market maker's total carryover position over the course of an option cycle is likely to grow quite large and may easily total thousands of contracts in complex spreads, even if few contracts are traded every day. There are several reasons for this inevitable growth.

First, a trader making markets in active months will be faced with a market that potentially has up to 50 or more option instruments differing by strike, month, and option type. One reason a large *inventory* of options accumulates over the course of an options cycle is simply that if a market maker can make a market in all option series, he or she will probably do so with enough capital to maximize profits. Over time, an active market maker's total carryover position will probably cover every strike that has an open interest. Second, an option carryover position is likely to grow larger with time because the market maker usually makes necessary continual small adjustments to correct for risk changes and *drift*.

But no matter how large or complex any option carryover position becomes, it will always resemble (on a single-month basis) one of the basic option positions in Table 4.1, irregular option positions not withstanding. An option trader should always know the exact type of the carryover option position, no matter how large or complex.

POSITION RISK PROFILES

Options differ from underlying assets in their exposure to risk. Financial assets or futures generally are only subject to positive or negative price change risk. Options also are subject to this risk as delta risk; in addition single-month options are exposed to gamma, theta, and kappa/vega risks. Options that include calendar spreads are exposed to all of these and to time delta and kappa/vega risk as well. The payoff at expiration and at 30 days and the delta, gamma, theta, and kappa/vega risk at 30 days are shown for selected single-month option positions in the Appendix to this chapter.

In Chapter 3 option risk was characterized by sign and dollar size for any small increment in instrument price, gamma, implied volatility, or time. But the sign and size of this risk may, and usually do, change as assets or futures price change. For example, a long call position may have a large negative theta in dollar terms at-the-money but a small negative theta either deep in- or out-of-the-money. A vertical spread may have positive theta at the short option strike but negative theta at the long option strike.

That option risks change as asset or futures prices change is termed the *risk modality* of the option. Each option position has its own risk modality for delta, gamma, theta, and kappa/vega. To quantify risk modality, one must measure risk over the extended range of futures prices over which options may continue to change value. This range must be at least six standard deviations wide to be able to capture extreme change.

The change in sign of risk in the basic single-month positions is reflected in the number of peaks (statistical modes) of gamma, kappa/vega, and theta risk (see Figure 4.2). No change in sign corresponds to one peak or mode, characteristic of single-option positions or straddles. A change in risk sign will be reflected in a twin-peaked risk (one positive and one negative) and is bimodal. A second change in risk sign results in a triple-peaked distribution and is trimodal.

These risk sign modes show that any spread risk is not equally proportional to the distribution of risk over a range of futures prices. Risk tends to gravitate to that strike option in a spread nearest to the futures price. The different modal peaks, then, just reflect the number of underlying spreads with different risk characteristics within a total position.

A single nonspread option or straddle position has unimodal kappa/vega, gamma, and theta risk profiles. Bi- or trimodality is introduced to risk any time any vertical spreads other than straddles are traded. Consider a simple bull spread in the figure on page 76, where gamma, kappa/vega, and theta risks have become bimodal. On the upside, a bull spread is positive theta and negative gamma and kappa/vega. On the downside, it is negative theta and positive gamma and kappa/vega. The two modes are positive or negative at the downside and upside strikes of the spread. Bimodality of gamma, kappa/vega and theta risk is also characteristic of other spreads, including fences, ratio spreads, and cartwheel positions.

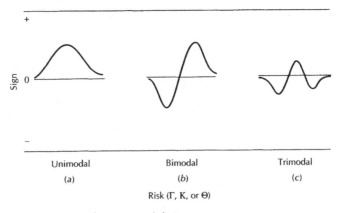

Figure 4.2   Risk sign modalities.

Butterfly and wrangle spread positions display trimodality of gamma, kappa/vega, and theta risk (figures on pages 82–83). The trimodality of the butterfly and wrangle strategies is an important feature in considering the optimal strategy to fit real market conditions (Chapter 7).

An *option position's risk profile* is composed of the simultaneous modalities of all risks–the delta, gamma, kappa/vega, and theta risk modalities and, if a calendar spread, the time delta and kappa/vega risk modalities as well. An option position's risk profile will uniquely identify that option position from all others, and will be critical in evaluating option strategies as trading vehicles.

For single-month option positions, several risk relationships are characteristic for gamma, kappa/vega, and theta. First, as with single option positions, gamma and theta are always of opposite sign but identical modality. Indeed, except for sign and an adjustment constant, gamma and theta are remarkably similar.

Second, for all single-month option positions, gamma and kappa/vega are always of the same sign, and each is opposite in sign to theta over all futures price ranges (Table 4.2). A trader is either long (positive) gamma and kappa/vega and short (negative) theta, or short (negative) gamma and kappa/vega and long (positive) theta. A trader who is *long volatility*, therefore, is also always negative theta in all single-month positions.

Third, gamma, kappa/vega, and theta risk have identical modalities in each single-month option position. If one knows any one risk sign and modality, one knows the signs and modalities of the other two risks. For example, if gamma is positive and unimodal, then kappa/vega is unimodally positive and theta is

Table 4.2 Sign of risk factors

Case I	*Case II*
Positive gamma	Negative gamma
Positive kappa/vega	Negative kappa/vega
Negative theta	Positive theta

unimodally negative. If gamma is trimodal, then kappa/vega is trimodal and of the same sign; and theta is trimodal and opposite in sign to gamma and kappa/vega.

Thus, if the sign and mode of any one of the non-delta risks are known, then the sign and mode of the other risks are known as well. In effect, there is really only one gamma/kappa/theta risk cluster (by sign and modality) in single-month positions, with gamma/kappa collapsing into one dummy (by sign) risk factor. For the statistically minded, there is only one degree of freedom.

The passage of time affects risk in single-month positions identically with single-option positions. In back-month positions kappa/vega is large while gamma and theta are low and wide. In front-month positions theta and gamma become larger although narrower while kappa/vega grows smaller and narrower in range. All long single-month positions grow more expensive to carry owing to time decay but are less affected by implied volatility change as time passes to expiration.

The interrelation of delta, gamma/theta, kappa/vega, and time risk modalities enormously simplifies option risk analysis of single-month option positions. Option positions now become strategic in which risk may be evaluated and not just measured, which is the topic of the next section.

LIMITED- AND UNLIMITED-RISK ANALYSIS

Theoretical consideration of option risks is validated only if it provides some practical guide to the relative risk exposure of the different option positions for trading purposes. Risk analysis must be both descriptive and evaluative. Previous sections have formally defined and quantitatively measured option risk profiles. In this section we begin to evaluate them.

For trading evaluation option positions must be divided between those that have limited- and those that have unlimited-risk exposure. A *limited-risk option* (LRO) position is one in which potential dollar loss is always finite and fixed in the worst-case risk scenario. Limited-risk exposure does not mean that dollar losses may not be large or severe, but only that they are fixed and finite no matter how large. The simplest LRO position is a long call or put.

An unlimited-risk option (URO) position has no fixed limit on the potential dollar loss in the worst-case risk outcome. Without a fixed limit on the amount of dollar loss that an option position may sustain in the worst-case scenario, risk is catastrophic. The potential dollar loss from an option position is unlimited and, therefore, could potentially be greater than the trader's entire capital, no matter how large. Unlimited risk is potentially catastrophic because it exposes the trader in the long run to bankruptcy. The simplest URO position is a short call or put.

Option risks such as rho, skew, or risks connected with expiration are almost always limited and will be considered in other chapters. But what are the limits on delta, gamma, theta, and kappa/vega risk? Which option risks are limited, and which are unlimited?

The delta risk is limited (or neutral) when delta converges asymptotically to zero change, or is positive on the upside and negative on the downside of the asset or futures price movement. The delta risk is unlimited when negative on the upside and positive on the downside, that is, the position loses unlimited money on either the upside or the downside.

The gamma and theta risks are limited whether they are positive or negative; they are always finite risks, no matter how large the loss. The same is not true for kappa/vega, however. There is no limit on the amount of profit/loss due to kappa/vega, and it is a potentially unlimited or catastrophic risk. In particular, it is usually a negative kappa/vega that is associated with unlimited-risk exposure in the case of an implied volatility blowout on the upside. Option positions which are negative kappa/vega, therefore, are unlimited-risk positions and generally poor strategy.

In normal markets, a positive kappa/vega risk exposure often is limited, although possibly large. In the event of a high implied volatility market, being positive with respect to kappa/vega might possibly represent an unlimited-risk situation should implied levels drop dramatically and fast. However, in normal markets, this risk should be limited. A market situation of high implied levels and positive kappa/vega will be taken up in Chapter 7.

A risk profile with a negative gamma, negative kappa/vega, and positive theta represents an unlimited-risk position. A positive gamma, positive kappa/vega, and negative theta risk profile constitutes a limited-risk exposure for single-month positions in normal markets, resulting primarily from the positive kappa/ vega risk stance. Of course, each of these asset-based risks also has a modality over a range of asset or futures prices. It is possible for an option position to be both limited and unlimited in delta or kappa/vega risk, depending upon the direction of asset prices. A short call, for example, has only a limited delta risk on the downside of asset prices but an unlimited risk on the upside. Its kappa/vega risk, however, is unlimited on both the upside and downside, reflecting the unimodal nature of single-option kappa/vega risk.

For most multi-option positions, however, kappa/vega risk is bi- or trimodal and may be both positive and negative over a range of futures prices. Kappa/vega risk, therefore, may be potentially both limited and unlimited. For purposes of initial risk evaluation, however, bi- or trimodal risk positions will be considered limited in kappa/vega risk (with normal volatility markets) if the number of options long in the total position is even with or greater than the number of short. As long as there is at least one long option to cover the risk of a short option, even negative kappa/vega risk in bi- or trimodal risk positions may be considered limited. The only single-month position in which this equal balance in long and short options may not limit risk is a fence, which will be the topic of a separate section in Chapter 7.

Table 4.3 summarizes the level of risk for the basic non–calendar-option positions. A URO position is subject to unlimited risk (U) in at least one direction of one risk in a risk profile. A LRO position only has limited risk (L) in both directions for all risks, or is a net even option spread.

Unlimited-risk option (URO) positions include the short call or put, short straddle/strangle and short ratio spreads, fences, and cartwheels. Some may be surprised to see a covered call position classified as a URO position, but a short call, long asset or future position is just a synthetic short put. A URO position may experience loss either as a result of an unlimited move in asset or futures prices or as a result of sudden increases in the implied volatility of option prices. A short straddle position may experience unlimited loss due to a delta extreme range move on limit days, and option prices may trade at extremely high implied volatility levels. In either case, the potential dollar loss is unlimited and catastrophic for those negative kappa/vega risks.

Table 4.3   Single-month option position risk summary
(∗ = unlimited risk)

Option Position	Delta	Gamma/Theta	Kappa/Vega
Unlimited risk position			
Short call or put	∗		∗
Short straddle/strangle	∗		∗
Bull and bear fence	∗		∗
Short ratio spread, calls, or puts	∗		∗
Short ratio spread, calls, and puts (short wrangle)	∗		∗
Bull or bear cartwheel	∗		∗
Limited risk position			
Long call or put			
Long straddle/strangle			
Bull or bear spread			
Long ratio spread, calls, or puts			
Long ratio spread, calls, and puts (long wrangle)			
Long or short butterfly/condor			
Synthetics			

Limited-risk option (LRO) positions include all the remaining positions except time spreads. These include the long options, long straddle/strangle, spreads and long ratio spreads, butterflies, long wrangles, and synthetics. All of these risks are limited bidirectionally in both delta and kappa/vega. Likewise, if one is in a spread position, risks are limited in either direction as long as the number of long options is equal to or greater than the number of short options in the total position. Some LROs are delta neutral and some are not.

The first prudent principle and strategic goal of every financial business is to avoid the risks of bankruptcy, even before consideration of profitability. It makes no sense to earn high profits if the likelihood of bankruptcy is still higher. This perspective toward risk will be referred to as the *prudent market-maker strategy* and represents the safe bet in the long run.

The strategies recommended in this text are of the limited-risk type. A prudently rational trader knows that any option strategy that is exposed to unlimited risk, no matter how small the probability, will eventually suffer catastrophe under the law of large numbers. As a Wall Street maxim notes, "There are bold traders and old traders but no bold, old traders."

Limited risk does not necessarily mean limited profits. Limited-risk option strategies may be highly profitable in several market situations—that is, those that are unprofitable to unlimited-risk traders! It is possible to have limited option risks yet unlimited profit potential. Prudent and informed market makers will strive to follow strategies that have these limited-risk/unlimited-reward characteristics.

A URO position resembles the risk exposure of a martingale gambling strategy, which increases the amount of the bet every time a loss occurs. In a series of losses, one could bet \$1, \$2, \$4, ... in a double-up martingale. If a gambler has sufficient capital and is content with modest profit, he or she may consistently earn money for long but limited periods of time with martingale strategies.

However, there eventually comes a series of consecutive-run losses that ultimately bankrupts the gambler. At that point, the gambler will no longer be able to play. For example, betting only a single dollar to start in a double martingale will bankrupt a gambler with a stake of less than \$255 within 1000 plays or so. Starting with only a dollar bet, a stake of \$1000 may expect to be wiped out in the course of over 4000 plays. There is no way in the long run to beat the odds consistently if they are against you. The improbable should never be assumed to be the impossible.

A naive option trader employing martingale strategies may make money for long periods before losing the entire stake in a rare or freak futures price run. This is the risk of the unlimited-risk option trader.

One could argue, of course, that the dollar loss on the short put is limited to a complete collapse of futures or asset prices, which is unlikely, and that it would still be a fixed loss. Indeed, the loss on a short put, at least in terms of intrinsic (delta) value, is limited. However, the value of the potential loss is catastrophically huge with most futures margins. Premium expansion for at-the-money options can easily reach $5000 per option in high implied volatility situations, and the margin required may increase exponentially.

Of course, at some level of capital (for example, $1 million or more) it may be possible to sell some small number of options net short and be exposed to negligible catastrophic risk. However, using $1 million of capital to short two or three options is probably not the optimum trading strategy, or use of margin or capital.

If the option speculator's profits are akin to gambling returns, then profits of limited-risk market makers may be considered similar to the returns to the house, that is, returns that take the opposite side of the bet from the gambler but that ultimately offset or hedge this bet with the bet of another gambler. The returns of the house (or market maker) come as a percentage of total wagers, whatever the side of the bet or the event outcome. (See Reichenstein and Davidson, 1987, for a gambling interpretation of option trading from the perspective of horse racing.)

RISK DETERMINATION

This section introduces a quick way to determine approximately the general limit of delta and kappa/vega risk of any single-month option position. (Time spread risk determination is taken up in Chapter 6). An option trader will always want to know what the exact risk profile is for each single-month carryover position at all times. Market-maker positions, however, have a tendency to grow larger during a complete cycle and include spreads covering every strike, with total carryover positions rising into the thousands. As we have already observed, any carryover position, no matter how large or complex, can be represented in one of the basic position types (Table 4.1); but identifying which one may require the use of option software (see Appendix).

Usually, a trader will have such option software available to perform this risk analysis on each cycle position. Nevertheless, a trader should be able to determine by hand calculation, without computer assistance, an approximate catastrophic risk profile for his or her carryover position. A trader may never have to do such manual calculations, but he or she should know how they are done.

Approximate single-month position, catastrophic risk exposure may be quickly estimated with some simple position numbers and calculations. There are three primary risk calculations: upside delta risk, downside delta risk, and kappa/vega risk. Consider futures options for illustration.

To calculate the potential upside delta risk, add the net total delta of the futures position and net call position, where each call carries the equivalent of one whole delta point.

$$\Delta \text{ upside risk } = \text{Net total futures } + \text{ Net calls}$$

If the result is positive, then the trader appears to have some limited upside delta risk, which is good. A negative delta would indicate potential unlimited risk.

To calculate the potential downside delta risk, add the net total of the futures position and the net put position, where each put carries the equivalent of one whole delta point.

$$\Delta \text{ downside risk } = \text{Net total futures } + \text{ Net puts}$$

If the result is negative, then the trader has a negative potential delta on the downside and is exposed only to limited risk. A positive downside delta exposure is an unlimited risk.

These risk calculations estimate upside and downside delta risk exposure but do not indicate a position's exposure to volatility risk. To approximate the position kappa/vega risk, add the net totals of calls and puts (long-positive), which gives net total options.

$$\text{Kappa/vega risk } = \text{Total net puts } + \text{ Net calls}$$
$$= \text{Net total options}$$

A positive total indicates that a position potentially has only limited kappa/vega risk in the event of a volatility explosion. A negative total indicates a position with unlimited-risk exposure. Consider the example of a single-month position shown in Table 4.4.

In this position, the delta upside risk is short 5, (short 10 futures and net long 5 calls). This result represents unlimited delta risk on the upside. Downside delta risk is short 30 (short 10 futures and net long 20 puts). The kappa/vega risk is long 25 options (net

Table 4.4 Hypothetical single-month position

Position	Subtotal
Long 10 130 calls	
Short 5 100 calls	
	(Net long 5 calls)
Short 20 100 puts	
Long 40 90 puts	
	(Net long 20 puts)
Short 10 futures	
	(Net short 10 futures)

long 5 calls and net long 20 puts), which is a positive kappa/vega exposure.

Summarizing this example, the upside delta risk is negative (unlimited), the downside delta risk is negative (limited), and the kappa/vega risk is positive (limited). This position risk profile resembles a bear cartwheel (see also the figure on page 81 in the Appendix to this chapter). Note that what is of importance is the number of options, in full delta points, rather than the dollar value of the net option position or its delta neutrality.

A trader must always know what the effect would be on the profit/loss of a position if futures prices were to experience a series of limit price moves on the upside or downside, or if implied volatility levels went from normal to high ranges (or from high to normal in high-volatility periods). If any of these trading events, no matter how unlikely, were to happen, would the position experience an unlimited loss? If the answer is yes, the position is catastrophically risk exposed.

These risk determinations are only approximate and may sometimes be deceptive, and of course they do not include time spread risks. What is often critical to the risk of a carryover position is the futures standard deviation between the constituent strike spreads. Obviously, a long 110 call may be a good delta hedge against a short 100 call if the standard deviation is 15 points, but not if it is only 2 points.

The risk determinations above also do not indicate the absolute dollar risk exposure by delta or kappa/vega, or the risk modalities, which are very important for position adjustment. For these reasons, option software analysis of position risk is almost indispensable. Nevertheless, a prudent trader should know how to do quick catastrophic risk determinations without such assistance.

APPENDIX: Position Risk Profiles—Selected Single-Month Positions

Positions		Positions	
1. Long Call	Buy 1 100 call	10. Long Call Ratio Spread	Short 1 100 call Long 2 105 calls
2. Short Call	Sell 1 100 call		
3. Long Put	Buy 1 100 put	11. Short Call Ratio Spread	Long 1 100 call Short 2 105 calls
4. Short Put	Sell 1 100 put	12. Bear Cartwheel	Long 1 100 call
5. Long Straddle	Buy 1 100 call Buy 1 100 put		Short 2 105 calls Short 1 100 put Long 2 95 puts
6. Short Straddle	Sell 1 100 call Sell 1 100 put	13. Long Butterfly	Short 1 100 call
7. Bull Spread	Buy 1 95 call Sell 1 105 call		Long 1 105 call Short 1 100 put Long 1 95 put
8. Bear Spread	Buy 1 105 put Sell 1 95 put	14. Long Wrangle	Short 1 100 call
9. Bull Fence	Buy 1 105 call Sell 1 95 put		Long 2 105 calls Short 1 100 put Long 2 95 puts

Where

Futures price	=	100
Day to Expiration	=	30
Implied Volatility	=	15
Interest Rate	=	10
1 Standard Deviation	=	5.7
2 SD	=	11.4

Scale Key:

A. $ = Dollar payoff at expiration (solid line) and at 30 days (light line).
B. Δ = Delta
C. Γ = Gamma
C. Θ = Theta
C. K = Kappa/Vega*

---

*Vega, of course, is not a Greek letter and therefore has no direct Greek alphabetical equivalent but in popular usage has become the substitute for kappa.

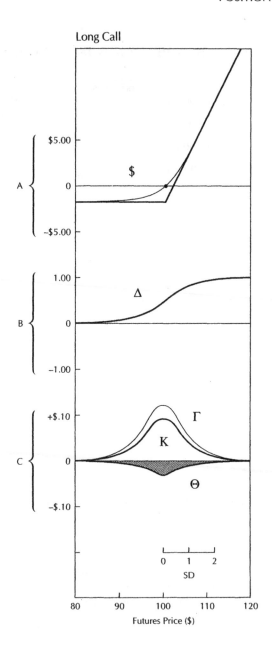

Short Call

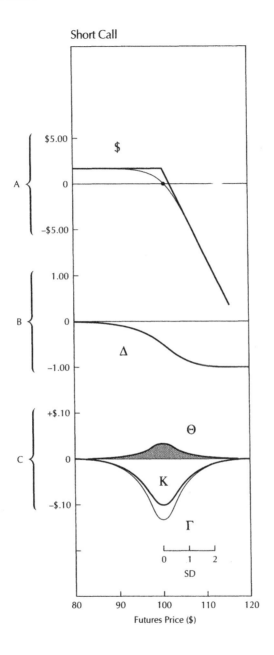

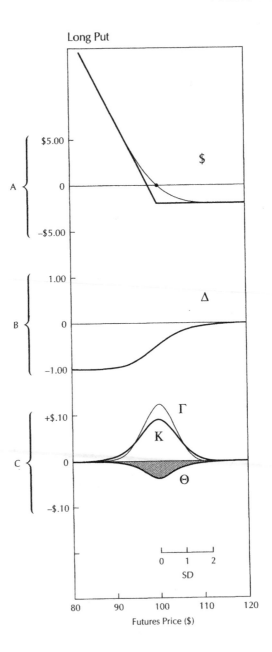

Short Put

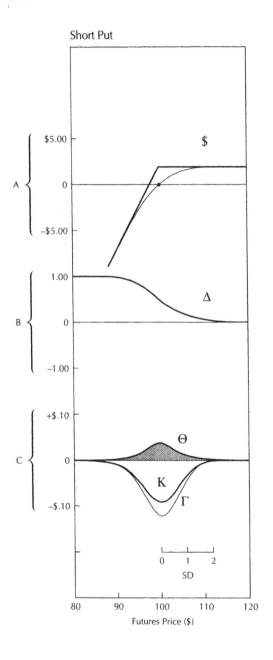

Long Straddle

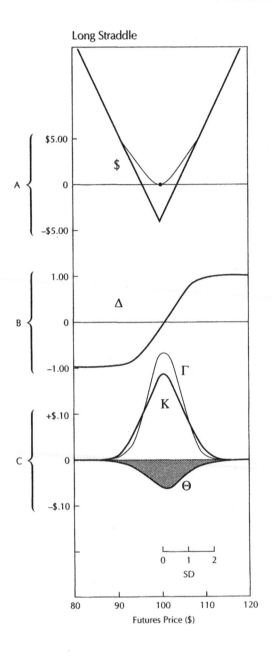

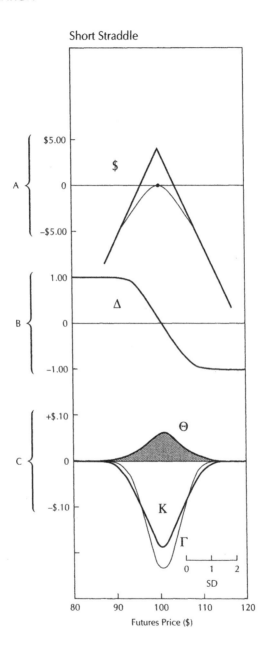

Bull Spread

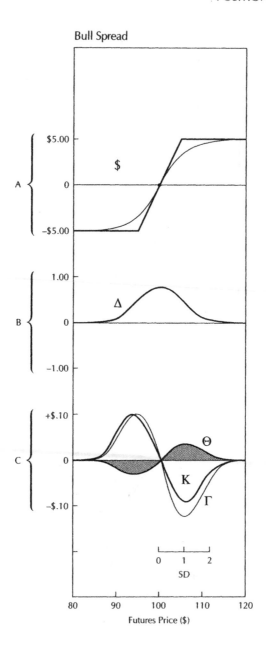

Bear Spread

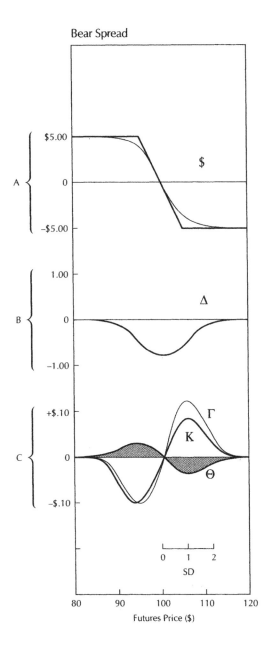

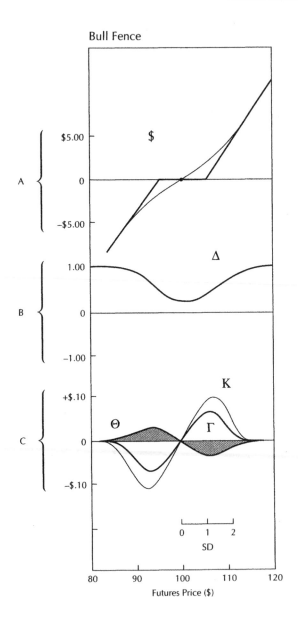

Bull Fence

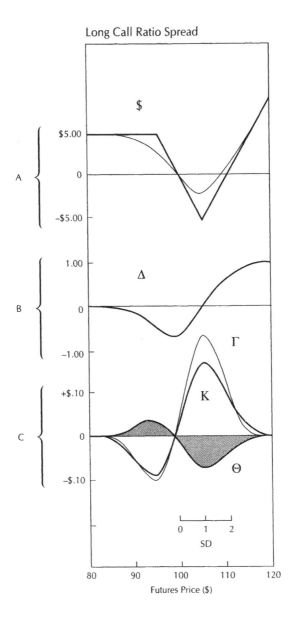

Long Call Ratio Spread

Short Call Ratio Spread

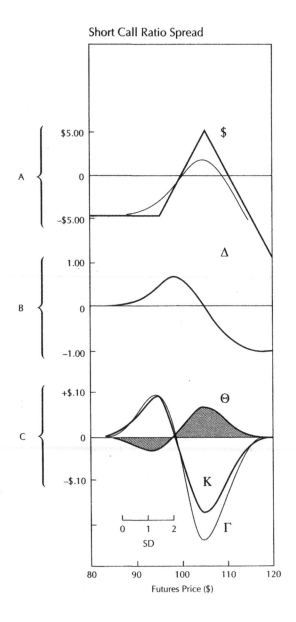

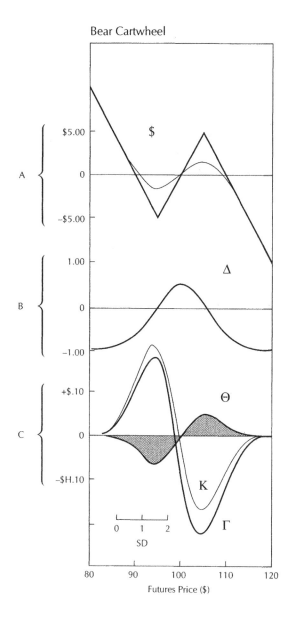

Bear Cartwheel

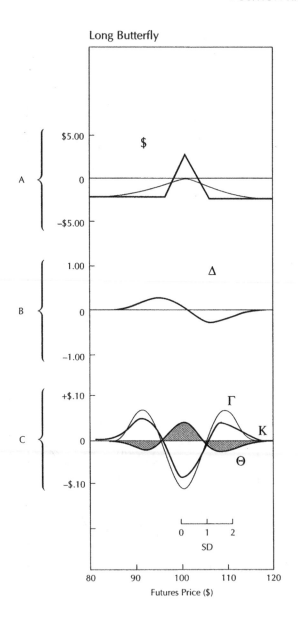

Long Butterfly

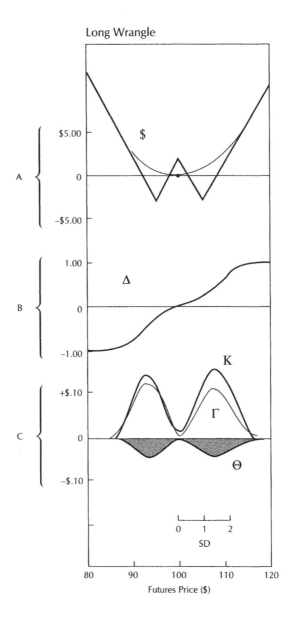

Long Wrangle

5

Synthetic Option Market Making

INTRODUCTION

Properly executed, synthetic option trades are virtually risk free and, therefore, represent the most risk conservative of all option trading. Synthetic trading is really a form of arbitrage, in which a discrepancy between the price of the actual option and its synthetic equivalent is captured as profit. Basic synthetic trading realizes an arbitrage profit in any same-month/same-strike call, put, and underlying asset.

Even if they are following other option strategies, option traders should be completely familiar with this form of trading, for synthetic principles will often determine which options are most appropriate for purchase or sale in any specific trading strategy. Trading synthetically does not require a fair-value option model, but such trading is almost uniformly impossible for off-floor option traders.

Synthetic arbitrage is based on the fact that a single-position long or short in any of the three trading instruments (call, put, asset) can be exactly duplicated by some combination of positions in the other two instruments. Any single long or short call, put, or asset contract position always has a synthetic equivalent value composed of a position in the other two option or asset contracts combined. The general put/call parity formula (Wong, 1991, p. 60) is:

$$P = C - S + \text{DF}(K)$$

where P = Price of put

             C = Price of call

             S = Current asset price

             K = Strike price

             DF( ) = Discounting function that calculates the net present value of the variable (in parentheses) at expiration

These parity relations are simplified for same-month and same-strike futures options in Table 5.1, disregarding for the moment

Table 5.1   Put/call/futures parity (same-month/same-strike)

Long call	= Long put and long future
Short call	= Short put and short future
Long put	= Long call and short future
Short put	= Short call and long future
Long future	= Long call and short put
Short future	= Short call and long put
Conversion	= Long future, short synthetic future
	(short call, long put)
	= Short call, long synthetic call
	(long put, long future)
	= Long put, short synthetic put
	(short call, long future)
Reversal	= Short future, long synthetic future
	(long call, short put)
	= Long call, short synthetic call
	(short put, short future)
	= Short put, long synthetic put
	(long call, short future)
Box	= Conversion and reversal at different strikes

the discounting function. Taking futures options as an example, a long call position is exactly equivalent to a long put of that same strike and a long futures contract, all of the same contract month. A long put and futures contract, therefore, is a long synthetic call. An option and its synthetic equivalent have not only the same delta payoff, but also the same gamma/kappa/theta risk profiles and, therefore, are risk-equivalent positions.

The strategy for trading synthetics is to take one side of an option position and the opposite side of its synthetic equivalent, so as to earn the price difference as profit. Knowing the price of any two same-strike/same-month options or futures, one can determine the price of the remaining option or future. These price relations between opposite options of the same strike/same month and underlying asset prices will be referred to as *synthetic parity* or *equal value*. Synthetic arbitrage takes advantage of differences in synthetic equal value prices.

Synthetic arbitrage is made up of *conversions, reversals,* or a combination of conversions and reversals known as *boxes.* Conversions and reversals are taken up in the next section and boxes in the subsequent section. For general illustration, the example of futures options will be used initially and then modified by consideration of financial asset discounts.

CONVERSIONS AND REVERSALS

A *conversion* is a long future, short call, long put position with all contracts at the same month (and strike). Equivalently, a conversion may be viewed as a long future/short synthetic future position, a short call/long synthetic call position, or a long put/short synthetic put position. A *reversal* (reverse conversion) is the exact opposite of the conversion: a short future, long call, and short put position. Thus, a holder of a conversion is always paired with a holder of reversal position.

A conversion or reversal is considered synthetically equal valued when the cost of the position is equal to the striking price of the options. For example, consider the following hypothetical prices: futures price at $104, a 100 call at $5 and a 100 put at $1 with all contracts of the same month. Since a conversion is a long future, short call, and long put, the cost of the conversion is $100 (= $104 − $5 + $1). That is, the cost of the futures' contract ($104) minus the sale of the call ($5) plus the cost of the put ($1) equals

$100. Since $100 is identical to the option strike (100), this conversion is synthetically equal valued at these prices. The calculation of the reversal position will give the same result.

To verify quickly that these prices are synthetically equal valued, consider this situation: If a trader bought the 100 call for $5 and simultaneously sold the 100 put for $1 and the future for $104, then no matter where the futures price settles at expiration, the trader's net profit will always be zero. Thus, if futures settle at 104, the trader will break even on the future contract, lose $1 on the time premium of the call (the call reflects only the intrinsic value of $4, not $5), and earn a profit of $1 on the 100 put as it expires worthless. The net result will be the same for any final futures settlement, not just 104, as one can easily verify with a quick calculation.

Procedures for computing synthetic equal values can be greatly simplified in practice. An in-the-money option should be synthetically equal valued to its same strike out-of-the money option when the time premium of the in-the-money option equals the time premium of the out-of-the-money option. In other words, option strike pairs are synthetically equal valued when the extrinsic, or time, value of each is the same. The only remaining difference in equal value between the strike pairs is intrinsic value.

Taking prices from the example above, one may quickly confirm this equivalence when futures are at 104:

	Extrinsic value	Intrinsic value	Total value
100 Call	$1	$4	$5
100 Put	$1	–	$1

When futures prices are at 104, the 100 call total value of $5 represents $4 of intrinsic value and $1 of extrinsic time value. The 100 put has no intrinsic value as an out-of-the-money option, but has $1 extrinsic time value. Since the time values of the call and put are identical ($1 = $1), they are synthetically equal valued to each other in this example. The steps in pricing the synthetic are summarized in Table 5.2.

When futures and options are synthetically equal valued (as in the above example) and can only be traded at those prices, then conversions and reversals offer no arbitrage profit. To obtain a synthetic profit in the previous example, the option trader must

Table 5.2   Pricing the synthetic

1. Calculate the intrinsic value (futures price − strike).

2. Set the out-of-the-money option price.

3. Add the intrinsic value to the out-of-the-money option price to find the same strike in-the-money option price.

Or

1. Follow Step 1 above.

2. Set the in-the-money option price.

3. Subtract the intrinsic value from the in-the-money option price to find the same strike out-of-the-money option price.

either sell the 100 call above $5, or buy the 100 put below $1, or both, assuming that futures contracts can be bought and sold at exactly 104. A trader will attempt to buy the underpriced time value option or sell the overpriced time value option synthetically and earn the difference as profit.

It is virtually impossible for a trader who is not on the trading floor to obtain synthetically profitable prices in option trades. This situation is not true for market makers. Not only must off-floor traders pay larger brokerage fees, but also, and more importantly, option prices need not be synthetically mispriced for floor market makers to earn arbitrage profits. Remember option prices are always quoted as either bid or offer prices. The average or settlement prices of options may be synthetically equal valued, but a market maker will always be buying somewhat below or selling somewhat above this exact equal-valued relation in the very course of making a market.

Using the example above in an actual option ring, one would find the 100 call is likely to be 4.90 bid at 5.10 offered, and the 100 put to be 0.90 bid and 1.10 offered. A trader could earn a maximum profit of 20 cents on a conversion or reversal by getting both sides of the edge on the put and call, $(5.10 − 5.00) + (1.00 − 0.90)$, provided futures prices could be bought or sold exactly at 104.

Ideally, a market maker wishes to sell options slightly above and buy options slightly below synthetic equal value in the course of making a market. In the activity of earning liquidity function profits, the market maker can conveniently use conversions and reversals to reduce risk significantly.

To complicate this picture for a synthetic trader, the opportunity to buy or sell futures exactly at 104 cannot be taken for granted, and indeed, may become problematic. There are several reasons why executing the futures part of a conversion or a reversal may affect the profits of the synthetic trade.

First, option market makers often do not execute the futures side of option hedges directly but use brokers even in situations where they could trade futures for themselves. Option traders often avoid leaving the options ring in order not to miss important trades or because it is not easy to do so in densely packed crowds of traders.

In using floor brokers, however, option traders must almost certainly expect to give up the edge to futures market makers, and pay a small brokerage fee as well (about $2 per contract). If options are traded in bid/offer spreads, so are futures contracts. It is not always possible to buy or sell futures contracts at exactly 104. Perhaps they can only be sold at 103.95 or bought at 104.05.

Second, option market makers may face problems if the synthetic options trades are based on slightly out-of-date futures prices. Depending upon where an option ring is located, option traders may not always know the latest quotations in the futures ring and must rely on board quotations, which are of necessity slightly delayed.

Third, particular futures contract months are sometimes less frequently traded, and price quotations may be particularly unreliable. In these months, market makers may be forced to rely upon their knowledge of futures price time spreads to estimate a futures' probable price.

All of these price-reporting delays and discrepancies can cause a market maker to misprice option synthetics slightly. Futures prices may be trading at 4.80 bid/4.90 offered and not the expected 4.90 bid/5.10 offered, at least not by the time an option trader wishes to complete the other side of a conversion or reversal in the futures ring.

To calculate the net profit owing to option arbitrage, one must subtract the cost of giving up the edge in the futures ring (in this example, 5¢), from the profit on both sides of the option trades (+20¢). If all goes well, then net profit is reduced but not eliminated. If futures prices are inaccurately assessed by option floor traders, then this arbitrage profit will be further reduced.

Option traders with a very large volume will often have clerks whose job is to signal futures pit prices directly to a trader before they are posted publicly, and if necessary these clerks give orders for market makers to brokers to execute futures trades. Although this up-to-date knowledge will reduce the loss from inaccurate futures prices when pricing synthetics, hiring a clerk will only be cost effective in large-volume markets.

Puts and calls do not always trade at exactly the same implied volatility. Sometimes a temporary market preference for calls in a rising market or puts in a falling market may send put and call prices out of line with their strike opposites. Contrarian technical traders may see this divergence as a barometer useful to predict a price direction contrary to the public market expectations. For whatever reason, however, wide disparities in the implied volatility levels of same-strike puts and calls mean that mispricing exists according to the synthetic parity formula.

If the market acts only from a directional sense in over- or undervaluing puts versus calls, the market is probably cheating itself by relying only on the purchase of one option and in so doing driving up time premiums relative to the other. A trader can always buy a synthetic put by buying a call and selling a future and obtain the same delta and kappa/vega risk. During a time of rising futures price trends, if the market is overvaluing calls relative to puts (or puts relative to calls in a falling market), an option market maker may take advantage of circumstances by selling the over-priced option and buying the underpriced synthetic equivalent. In this situation a general rule of thumb is to buy calls (and sell the synthetic) in a falling market, and to buy puts (and sell the synthetic) in a rising market.

A market maker must be totally familiar with trading synthetics and with the rule of value parity and risk equivalence between an option and its synthetic. If a trader is able to make quick calculations of synthetic price relations, he or she can earn a liquidity profit without knowing anything else about options. Even without a fair-value model (characteristic of markets before the BSM model) one can still trade and make a market in options using synthetic equivalence.

To simplify the repetitive calculations of the relative values of options and synthetics, market makers frequently have recourse to printed fair-value option tables that list the values of puts and calls over a range of futures prices with specified risk assumptions. With such a table the practiced trader can easily see at a glance which options are not trading exactly at equivalent fair values, or which options should be bought or sold. Table 5.3 is an example of a fair-value option table.

Table 5.3 Fair value option table

Futures option value table		03-28-1991				Futures settlement = 100.00				©EPSILON		C Call value/Delta
Any/May		Interest rate = 10.00%				Days to expire = 30				OPTIONS		P Put value \ Delta
Volatility =		15.0/	15.0/	15.0/	15.0/	15.0/	15.0/	15.0/	15.0/	15.0/	15.0/	15.0/
Future strike		90	92	94	96	98	100	102	104	106	108	110
110.00	C[a]	20.00/99	18.00/99	16.00/99	14.00/99	12.00/.99	10.02/99	8.07/96	6.21/91	4.50/81	3.03/67	1.87/50	110.00
	P	0.00\0	0.00\0	0.00\0	0.00\0	0.00\0	0.02\1	0.07\4	0.21\9	0.50\19	1.03\33	1.87\50	
105.00	C	15.00/99	13.00/99	11.01/99	9.03/98	7.10/95	5.28/88	3.66/76	2.33/59	1.34/41	0.70/27	0.33/16	105.00
	P	0.00\0	0.00\0	0.01\0	0.03\2	0.10\5	0.2\12	0.66\24	1.33\41	2.34\59	3.70\73	5.33\84	
100.00	C	10.01/99	8.04/98	6.14/93	4.38/83	2.88/69	1.70/50	0.91/33	0.43/21	0.18/11	0.06/6	0.02/3	100.00
	P	0.01\1	0.04\2	0.14\7	0.38\17	0.88\31	1.70\50	2.91\67	4.43\79	6.18\89	8.06\94	10.02\97	
95.00	C	5.20/90	3.53/78	2.16/60	1.18/41	0.57/25	0.24/14	0.09/7	0.03/4	0.01/0	0.00/0	0.00/0	95.00
	P	0.20\10	0.53\22	1.16\40	2.18\59	3.57\75	5.24\86	7.09\93	9.03\96	11.01\99	13.00\99	15.00\99	
90.00	C	1.53/50	0.75/31	0.32/18	0.12/9	0.04/5	0.01/0	0.00/0	0.00/0	0.00/0	0.00/0	0.00/0	90.00
	P	1.53\50	2.75\69	4.32\82	6.12\91	8.04\95	10.01\99	12.00\99	14.00\99	16.00\99	18.00\99	20.00\99	
May		90	92	94	96	98	100	102	104	106	108	110	May

Futures option value table Any/July	03-28-1991 Interest rate = 10.00%					Futures settlement = 100.00 Days to expire = 60				©EPSILON OPTIONS	C Call value/Delta P Put value \ Delta
Volatility =	15.0/	15.0/	15.0/	15.0/	15.0/	15.0/	15.0/	15.0/	15.0/	15.0/	15.0/
Future strike	90	92	94	96	98	100	102	104	106	108	110
110.0 C[a]	20.00/99	18.00/99	16.01/99	14.03/99	12.07/97	10.16/94	8.33/90	6.62/83	5.07/74	3.73/62	2.62/50
P	0.00\ 0	0.00\ 0	0.01\ 0	0.03\ 1	0.07\ 3	0.16\ 6	0.33\10	0.62\17	1.07\26	1.73\38	2.62\50
105.00 C	15.01/99	13.03/99	11.08/97	9.19/93	7.39/88	5.73/80	4.27/69	3.03/56	2.06/44	1.33/33	0.82/25
P	0.01\ 1	0.03\ 1	0.08\ 3	0.19\ 7	0.39\12	0.73\20	1.27\31	2.03\44	3.06\56	4.33\67	5.82\75
100.00 C	10.10/96	8.22/92	6.47/85	4.88/76	3.51/64	2.39/50	1.55/38	0.96/29	0.56/20	0.30/13	0.16/ 8
P	0.10\ 4	0.22\ 8	0.47\15	0.88\24	1.51\36	2.39\50	3.55\62	4.96\71	6.56\80	8.30\87	10.16\92
95.00 C	5.57/82	4.06/71	2.80/57	1.82/43	1.12/32	0.65/23	0.35/15	0.18/ 9	0.09/ 6	0.04/ 4	0.02/ 3
P	0.57\18	1.06\29	1.80\43	2.82\57	4.12\68	5.65\77	7.35\85	9.18\91	11.09\94	13.04\96	15.02\97
90.00 C	2.15/50	1.33/37	0.77/26	0.41/17	0.21/11	0.10/ 6	0.04/ 4	0.02/ 3	0.01/ 0	0.00/ 0	0.00 0
P	2.15\50	3.33\63	4.77\74	6.41\83	8.21\89	10.10\94	12.04\96	14.02\97	16.01\99	18.00\99	20.00\99
July	90	92	94	96	98	100	102	104	106	108	110 —July

[a]C = call; P = put.

93

This basic principle of making conversions or reversals is the essence of synthetic trading. Synthetic option relationships offer the astute market maker frequent opportunities for small bid/offer spread and arbitrage profits. Unlike stock option synthetical trading, futures options need not consider the effect of dividends on synthetic trading. However, the discussion so far of trading conversions and reversals has assumed that there exist no costs of carry or capital opportunity costs. That is, interest rates are zero. Since this is not the case in the real financial world, we shall consider in the next section how interest rates affect synthetic arbitrage.

THE EFFECT OF INTEREST RATES ON SYNTHETIC TRADING

The BSM formula requires that interest rates be used to discount the option fair value in order to reflect the opportunity cost of capital, or the cost of carry. The specific relationship of cost of carry to option value varies depending on whether the underlying asset is a bond, stock, currency, spot commodity, or futures contract. Depending on the economic features of the underlying asset, the cost of carry will be either positive or negative, or even zero. For positive cost-of-carry assets, such as stocks, an increase in the interest or dividend rate will raise the value of the call and decrease the value of the same-strike put as the implicit forward stock price rises (see Cox and Rubinstein, 1985). In the bond market, both positive and negative cost-of-carry markets are possible, depending on the time spreading of a bond position relative to the term structure of interest rates (Bookstaber, 1987; Wong, 1991). In futures markets, where the current futures price is the forward price and contains the implicit cost of carry, option values are affected less by futures cost of carry than by the cost of carry of the option position itself. Option traders should be familiar with the cost-of-carry considerations in the underlying financial or commodity market in which they are trading. The following discussion of interest rates and synthetic values will be limited to futures options.

The fact that options must be positively or negatively discounted means also that the synthetic parity formula in the previous section will not always hold before expiration. In other words, in actual market conditions options often do not trade at the pure synthetic basis because of different costs of carry of the option position itself. Synthetic trading is an interest-rate arbitrage as well as a put/call arbitrage.

The interest-rate arbitrage of synthetic trading extends to the financing of the futures option position itself, exclusive of the cost of carry of the underlying asset. When at- or near-the-money strike synthetics are traded, interest rates do not play much part in altering the synthetic parity formula. This lack of influence arises because the cost of carry will be almost the same for both sides of the strike. That is, to buy an at-the-money call and to sell the put will be done for even money.

The same is not true for wing strike synthetics, since on the wings there is a large difference in the cost of carry, with one option deeply in-the-money and the other out-of-the-money. Except for at-the-money conversions and reversals, one side or the other of a synthetic will always have a larger value and, thus, a larger absolute discount than the other. That one side of a synthetic has a larger value/discount than the other means that the parity formula must be discounted by the cost of carry to the buyer or seller.

Consider a situation where interest rates are 12 percent, futures are trading at 100, and the value of the 90 put is 0.50, or 50 cents, with 30 days to expiration. Without interest rates, the extrinsic value of the 90 put and 90 call must be equal, so that the 90 call would be worth 10.50 (10 intrinsic and 0.50 extrinsic). With a 12 percent annualized interest rate over one-month cost of carry (1 percent), the value of the 90 call would be reduced by 10.5 cents to approximately 10.40. This reduction will mean that the synthetic 90 put (call and future), will be worth only 40 cents. The synthetic put at 0.40 cents, therefore, is worth less than the actual 90 put trading at 0.50 cents. Generally, the out-of-the-money synthetic equivalent will almost always trade at some discount to the corresponding actual option.

The discount to the more expensive option in a synthetic position need not be the full cost of carry, however. For a synthetic position, the cost of carry is a function of the net debit/credit, not the debit/credit on the more expensive option alone. If the 90 put is selling for $4 when futures are at 100, then the synthetic parity value of the 90 call is $14 ($10 intrinsic and $4 extrinsic). The net debit/credit of the 90 synthetic (put and call), therefore, is just $10 and not $14. With a 1 percent one-month cost of carry, the 90 call will be discounted at 0.105 again, but this time taken from $14. Thus, the synthetic value of the discounted 90 call should be about 13.90. That is, the synthetic 90 put should trade at $3.90 ($4 − $0.10), versus the actual 90 put at $4. In summary, the discount to the more expensive option in a synthetic trade is taken from the intrinsic value only, since the extrinsic value of both options in a synthetic will be equal.

From these discount relations, one can formulate a tactical goal of attempting to hold undervalued debit synthetics and sell overvalued credit synthetics, each value being determined relative to the cost of carry of the full synthetic position. The most nearly ideal situation would be to sell the in-the-money option at the full nondiscounted synthetic value and buy the actual option. By doing this, a trader will have established a net credit position that earns risk-free interest for the trader. Essentially, this goal entails doing in-the-money call and out-of-the-money put conversions and in-the-money put and out-of-the-money call reversals.

To pursue this strategy in the most prudent way, the smart trader is always on the lookout to keep a large inventory of long out-of-the-money options against which large synthetic credit trades may be made at any time. To attempt to *leg* the synthetic by selling the in-the-money option first, and then looking to buy the actuals may be too risky if for some reason the actual wings cannot be bought or become overpriced.

Although earning the interest rate on doing credit synthetics may seem like a small rate of return, the income so derived can be highly leveraged by the use of margin. Option margin is somewhat different on each commodity or futures exchange, but there is a tendency to accept the principles of *delta margining*. The process of delta option margining essentially uses net delta plus the number of options held to determine margin. The margin may sometimes be as low as several hundred dollars per option for synthetically spread options.

Since credit synthetics can usually be done for a net credit of many hundreds or thousands of dollars, the rate of interest on the synthetic credit may easily equal the margin in the best-case outcome. Thus, the rate of interest on the credit will not represent the true rate of return to capital, but will greatly underestimate it. For this reason, this net credit synthetic trading strategy is recommended whenever possible.

Nevertheless, even though a net credit synthetic position is a good strategy, it is not perfect. For instance, deep in-the-money options do not trade so frequently as deep out-of-the-money options, and the number of synthetics that can be completed is thus limited. Also, although a net credit may be put on when doing a synthetic, it is possible that asset price moves may subsequently turn the net credit to a net debit with a negative cost of carry! This situation would develop if asset prices moved down against a conversion holder, or up for a reversal holder. In these cases, the positive cost of carry would become negative. This problem, however, is overcome if a trader is able to execute a combination of conversions and reversals known as a *box*, discussed in the next section.

BOX ARBITRAGE

When a trader completes a conversion and a reversal for different strike pairs but of the same month, he or she has completed a *box*. When a conversion (long future, short call X, long put X), is completed in conjunction with a diferent strike reversal (short future, long call Y, short put Y), only the net option position remains, because the long and short futures positions cancel each other out. Whereas conversions and reversals separately always require some futures position, boxes do not (see Figure 5.1).

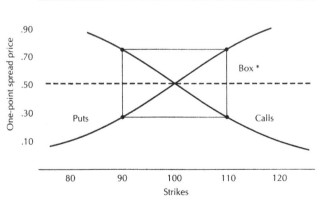

* Box prices assume single put and call prices. Other prices are
  based on one point strike spread. Futures = 100.

Figure 5.1 Put and call spread and box prices.

In doing boxes, it is appropriate to use any spread between the strikes of the conversion and reversal. A box may be done equally well on the 95–96 strike spread as on the 95–105 strike spread. *Jellyrolls* resemble boxes except that they are done horizontally in time, with a conversion/reversal in one month offset by a reversal/conversion in another month.

In looking for box trades, a market maker needs to be familiar with the vertical spread market for puts and calls. Spreads at the same strikes between puts and calls, when added, must equal the distance of the strikes. For a single whole point strike spread, for example, if the 100–101 put spread is trading for .55, then the 100–101 call spread will be equal valued at .45 with the synthetic box value summing to one point. In other words, knowing the value of an option spread of one option type, one can determine the synthetic spread fair value of the other option type for the same strikes.

An option trader should always be on the lookout for basic synthetic, box, or spread arbitrage profits. However, not all synthetic or box positions may be equally desirable. As we noted in the previous section, trading net credit synthetics offers a leveraged interest rate income in addition to normal scalping. For these reasons, all boxes should not be considered the same.

Ideally, a market maker trading synthetics as a net credit strategy would like to sell in-the-money options and buy out-of-the-money options. Practically, the trader must do conversions with deep in-the-money (short) calls and reversals with deep in-the-money (short) puts. By being long out-of-the-money calls and long out-of-the-money puts, a trader will show a credit balance on which interest may be earned. The optimum risk-free option position is to hold a conversion at strikes below futures price, and a reversal on strikes above future prices. This position will represent a net credit box spread. Obviously, the opposite position (doing reversals with in-the-money calls and conversions with in-the-money puts) is the least profitable synthetic strategy if the goal is to earn an interest income.

For a trader who is doing synthetics and attempting to create a balanced box, the number of futures contracts held long or short relative to the number of option contracts in the total synthetic position is a good indicator of the degree of balance for the box achieved. An optimum box, even one covering hundreds of contracts spread over all different strikes, need contain no futures contract positions in it at all.

PIN RISK

In a conversion, reversal, or box, the option trader is not subject to any of the major risks considered in Chapter 3 (skew, delta, kappa/vega or theta). Synthetics are virtually risk-free positions and, therefore, are generally considered the most conservative form of option trading.

Nevertheless, there are some risks associated with synthetic trading of which an option trader should be aware. Aside from the trading risk of completing synthetics, there is some very slight degree of rho risk since synthetic parity values will be affected by a change in interest rates as noted in the previous sections. There are two other risks that also deserve mention: expiration (*pin*) risk and inefficient market risk. Pin risk is taken up in this section and inefficient market risk in the next.

There are two forms of option exercise at expiration: futures/ asset and cash settled. Most options exercise a right to purchase or sell a futures/asset contract at or before the expiration date on the call/put (futures/asset-settled). The option and futures/asset do not have the same expiration, and the futures/asset continues to trade after the option expires. Thus, a May orange juice call is a right to buy a May futures contract up to the call's expiration in April, while the May future continues to trade into May itself.

A cash-settled option expiration occurs when both the option and the futures/asset stop trading on the same expiration date and all cycle accounts are settled in cash differences. Since both expire on the same day, there is no longer a future/index contract for that month. Stock index options and stock index futures options (S&P 100; S&P futures and options, and so on), are the notable form of cash expiration on a quarterly basis (the *triple witching hour*). Stock index futures and options recently have introduced a form of futures-settled option expiration for off-quarter months. The December option is cash settled, but the January option is futures settled, for example.

From the standpoint of synthetic trading the most risk-free approach is a cash settlement option expiration, because there is no uncertainty about exercise if the underlying instrument expires in cash. Futures-settled or other financial options, however, carry some risk at expiration. If futures settle near the exercise strike at expiration the opposite trader may not exercise the short side of the synthetic. This situation is known as pin risk, since a synthetic holder may be *pinned* to the strike and future at expiration.

A long option holder may choose not to exercise at expiration even if the option is in-the-money. Consider a situation where futures settle at 100.20 on the last option-trading day and a trader holds long 100 calls. Will a long-call holder always exercise at this price? Not necessarily. Although the long-call holder will hold a call worth $0.20 in intrinsic value on expiration day, this profit may be realizable only if futures can be sold for 100.20. The critical unknown facing the long-option holder is how much the futures prices will change on the opening of trading on the next day after the expiration day settlement. In the above example, if futures prices should open below 100 on the next trading day, then the profit on the long call will not be realized if exercised.

Since many off-floor option traders must pay a higher brokerage fee than floor traders and are not always constantly in touch with the market, some long-call holders will not exercise options that are in the money by only some small amount on expiration.

Somewhat paradoxically, a long-option holder may choose to exercise a slightly out-of-the-money option at expiration. Options do not have to be in-the-money to be exercised. This may be done, for example, if the holder wished to acquire the futures position without having to trade for futures in the futures pit. Taking delivery on futures contracts (long or short) via slightly out-of-the-money options may help large traders who, perhaps because of size or market liquidity considerations, wish to take a large position in futures without introducing new demand into the futures ring itself.

In summary, a long-option holder may not exercise a small in-the-money option at expiration if the profit is too small relative to the risk of futures price change at the opening of trade on the first post-expiration day. Also, a long-option holder may exercise slightly out-of-the-money options from time to time.

The problem that these uncertainties pose to synthetic traders with futures-settled exercise is the overnight uncertainty of their actual position. Consider the situation where a market maker holds conversions at 100 (short 100 calls, long 100 puts, long futures) when futures settle at 100.20 on expiration day. If the long 100 call option holder exercises against the short 100 call market maker, then the market maker surrenders the long futures and carries no position on the day after expiration. But if the long

100 call trader does not exercise for some reason, then the market maker will carry over an unintended long futures position on the day after expiration.

Thus, the synthetic trader will not know whether he or she will be exercised against on the short side of the synthetic until after it is possible to do anything about it. This situation creates a period of time at expiration when there is risk exposure in a directional price move overnight. At expiration the synthetic holder of an at- or nearly in-the-money strike will be subject to windfall losses (or profits) from time to time.

Although one or two contract synthetics exposed to pin risk will not matter, having a large synthetic position at the strike closest to futures prices on expiration day poses an appreciable risk of unintended long or short futures carryover on the day after expiration for most market makers. Of course, there is also the possibility of windfall profits in futures-settled options, but this is always the other side of risk. A market maker will generally be interested in neutralizing risk, not speculating on it.

There is no perfect protection against pin risk in doing synthetics in futures-settled options. The most adventagous way to avoid this risk is to cross a conversion with a reversal of the same strike, and market makers may wish to check with other floor traders who want to get out of synthetics at expiration. Of course, finding a match is not always possible, and most market makers will often find themselves on the same side of the synthetic. Thus, the synthetic holder may be unable to avoid carrying pin risk into expiration.

In this situation, a market maker must make an educated guess about how many short small in-the-money options he or she will be exercised against. Although one might assume that all in-the-money options will be exercised at expiration, surprisingly this assumption is not always true. In practice, as much as half or even more of short options with small profit margins may not be exercised, but this percentage will obviously decline steeply as the option moves more into the money at expiration.

Expiration-related risk can only affect one option strike synthetic per expiration. Therefore, this risk will usually affect only a small percentage of a market maker's total position, since rarely will a total position be at one strike. Although pin risk is not a catastrophic option risk, the absolute amount at risk may be high and worthy of attention.

INEFFICIENT MARKET RISK

A conversion or reversal is generally risk-free if the underlying call, put, and future are trading in a reasonably efficient market. Ideally, in an efficient market the relative synthetic fair values of synthetic options are priced within a bounded range. Practically, however, the same strike/month put and call may not trade at synthetic equal value equivalence. Such a market would be inefficient, and could pose some monetary risk to synthetic positions, at least until fair price relations came back into line.

The risk to the synthetic trader is that one side of the option synthetic will become drastically over- or undervalued in the absence of corrective market response. Although price inefficiencies are rare, they are not impossible. There are several ways in which such inefficiencies may affect synthetic option price relations.

Virtually all futures exchanges enforce some sort of limits on the maximum daily change in a futures contract (except possibly for the spot month near expiration). But not all exchanges have rules to limit daily price moves in options. Since a synthetic or reversal is composed of both options and a future, it is possible there will be times when synthetic price relations may not be synthetically fair valued on those exchanges with different limit restrictions on price changes in futures and options.

Consider a situation in a non–limit-restricted market where futures prices may fall from 100 to 96 on a given day. If there is a two-point daily price limit restriction imposed, futures prices will fall the limit to 98 and must settle there. If the option market continues to trade without limit, however, option prices may reflect actual futures market conditions and trade as if futures prices were at 96 (and not the 98 limit). In this situation, a large price distortion may appear in synthetic price relations. For example, assume that a trader holds a reversal (short futures, long calls, and short puts). If futures prices settle at the 98 limit, but option prices reflect futures prices of 96, the reversal holder will suffer a major loss at settlement, since his or her long call and short put have caused more losses than were matched by gains in the short futures. In effect, the gain on the real short futures does not offset the loss in the synthetic long future. Conversely, a conversion holder would experience a windfall profit in this example, equal to the loss of the reversal holder.

If the limit on a price move is on the order of $1000 per synthetic on an option exchange, then a large synthetic holder could be exposed to six-figure profit-and-loss swings on a limit day. Generally, reversal holders will suffer losses on downside futures limit days while conversion holders will show profits. On upside limit days, reversal holders may show windfall profits to conversion holder losses.

The losses on these synthetics (a reversal on a down limit day and a conversion on an up limit day) would only exist on paper, however, until the market came off limit (open trading resumed) and thus cannot be realized in any way. As long as futures prices eventually do come off limit, the losing side of the synthetic position will also eventually come out even again. Under no circumstances should a downside reversal and an upside conversion holder attempt to trade out of only one spread side of their positions, for there is no risk at expiration or when futures prices come off limit. To attempt to do otherwise is to risk locking in unnecessary losses.

A more serious risk for synthetic traders as well as others could come about in the event of a general market financial crisis, in which clearinghouses experience financial difficulties (see Chapter 3). A suspension of guarantees to an option trader that results in a forced liquidation of an option position can have serious financial consequences even to synthetic traders. If a trader believes that his or her clearinghouse is at risk of default, he or she should attempt to transfer (ex pit) his or her position to another house.

6

Calendar Spread Risk

INTRODUCTION

To hold *a calendar spread* is to hold one option position in one month and at the same time a second option position in another month. A calendar spread is also known as a *horizontal* or *time spread*. The universe of two-legged time spread positions is 400 (20 × 20), since each possible single-month position (of which there are approximately 20) may be spread theoretically with any other position in a time spread. Adding a third month (leg) to the spread would create a time butterfly, with a theoretical universe of 8000 possible variants. Since only a small fraction of these possible time spreads have been considered in options studies, there is likely much to be learned about time spread risk.

Many traders assert that initiating a time spread is one way to reduce or neutralize the delta and kappa/vega risks in any single-month position. Maybe. The most commonly recommended time spread strategy is to short kappa/vega in one month against long kappa/vega in another month, usually with the front-month short and the back-month long in what may be called a *short kappa/vega time strategy*.

The simplest short time position is a one-to-one ratio at the same strike or strike futures basis. But other variations are possible such as *diagonal spreads*, in which the strikes are not the same, or other more complex combinations. In all of these strategies, however, the delta and short kappa/vega risks of one month option are offset by the delta and long kappa/vega of another month option. All these calendar positions will here be termed short kappa/vega time strategies, whether the short time leg is the front or back-month.

In financial markets especially, where asset time spreads are driven by the cost of carry, short option time spreads are an important component of any large option portfolio. The short kappa/vega time option strategies resemble the long front/short back-month futures strategy, which seeks to capture a positive cost of carry in this time position. The silver futures time spread market has long been used to capture this positive cost of carry (or interest), and the strategy dates back to the nineteenth-century metals markets (Wolff, 1987).

If one takes the total combined net delta and the total net kappa/vega of the two-legged time position, the risk may approximate zero according to the definition of single-month position risk. Indeed, it even may be possible to be both positive theta and positive kappa/vega in a total time position, which it is impossible to do in a single-month position. This reduction or improvement of delta and kappa/vega risk through calendarization conforms to the popular impression that time spread trading is a limited-risk strategy *if* single-month theta and positive kappa/vega are the appropriate measures of risk.

Despite its supposed advantage or necessity, time spreading may be more risky than perceived. Market makers who use time spreading as a risk reduction strategy may be deceiving themselves, for any time spread reduction in the delta and kappa/vega risks may come at the cost of increasing potential exposure to other time-based risks, which may be as large as or larger than the risks just reduced.

Time spreading exposes traders to the new risks of time delta and time kappa/vega, as defined below. It is time-based delta risk and time-based kappa/vega risk that determine the riskiness of option time spreads, not delta and kappa/vega risk as defined for single-month positions.

As with single-month risk, time risks may be considered limited or unlimited. Generally, the short kappa/vega time strategies are exposed to unlimited or catastrophic risk, but other time strategies that effectively limit time risk are possible. Only after the reader has grasped the concept of time risk and its limits, discussed in this chapter, should he or she move on to Chapter 7 and its formulation of option market-making strategies as a whole.

TIME DELTA (Δ) RISK

Time delta is simply the risk to a futures option time spread due to a change in the futures price time spread basis. Only futures options time spreads are subject to time delta risk.

$$\text{Time } \Delta = \frac{\text{Dollar change in option time spread value}}{\text{Dollar change in futures price time spread}}$$

For example, assume that a trader is short the 100 May call at $1.70 with a 15 implied volatility level with 30 days to expiration, and long the 100 June call at $2.39 at the same implied level with 60 days to expiration, with both the May and June futures at 100. If the May future goes to 101 while the June future stays at 100 (all else being equal), the May call will go from $1.70 to $2.25, a change of +$0.55. This $0.55 will represent a loss to the short May call/long June call time spread and is the time delta risk. The payoff profile and futures basis risk delta are shown in Figure 6.1.

The short front-month/long back-month call spread is negative time delta for all futures basis moves between futures prices 90 and 110. That is, the position will always lose money if the futures spread between the front and back goes backward. The time futures basis delta of a position has no mode and resembles the delta of a short call. It is not the same, however, as the total position delta, which is bimodal (put side positive, call side negative) and resembles the delta of a long butterfly single-month position. But it is precisely because total position delta gives a reassuring risk perspective that time futures basis delta grows in importance.

Only futures options are subject to time delta risk because generally only futures have a time basis spread in the underlying asset. Stock or cash financial calendar options are exercisable against the same fixed asset, whereas futures options by month are exercisable only against the future of the corresponding month. A futures basis price spread becomes a direct risk to any time spread futures option strategy. Since there is virtually no theoretical limit to the basis of futures monthly spreads, except

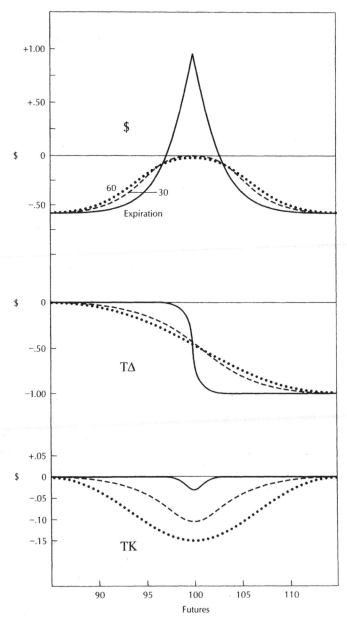

Figure 6.1 Time risks for a short front-month/long back-month case. Expiration refers to front-month option.

perhaps the worthlessness of the future contract itself, time delta risk may pose a potential for catastrophic loss to a futures option position that is improperly hedged.

While time delta risk poses a serious risk to calendar option positions, it may reasonably be offset or hedged by executing a futures time spread to neutralize the delta of the option time spread for each month separately. For a short front/long back call spread, for example, a trader would go long front-month futures and short back-month futures so as to execute a standard hedge against commodity inventory, albeit an inventory of options. This action will partially protect the total option position from futures price basis.

When the net delta spread of the option position is reversed in an offsetting equivalent delta spread in the futures market, time delta risk is reduced considerably, and futures spreading is always recommended for prudently hedged futures options time spreads. To the extent that option time spreads are delta-neutral for each month separately, time delta risk may be limited.

Unfortunately, using futures markets to hedge time delta risk to option spreads properly will cost market makers extra money and lower the profitability of the original option spread. Although avoiding the futures spread to protect the option time spread will save money in the short run, it will only expose the trader to very large losses in the long run and is a mistake in strategy. For nonfutures option time spreads, of course, neither futures basis nor time delta risk exists. Woe be it to the stock option trader, however, who trades futures options in the same way as stock options.

TIME KAPPA/VEGA (K) RISK

Both futures and cash options calendar spreads are also subject to risk of change in the level of implied volatility in each leg of the spread, regardless of futures price spread change. This risk may be defined as:

Time K (or Vega)

$$= \frac{\text{Dollar change in option time spread}}{\text{One-point increase in time implied volatility spread}}$$

Reconsider the option strategy of a short front-month call and long back-month call of the same strike with the calendar futures price basis at zero. Front- and back-month options do not necessarily trade at similar implied volatilities. The market may estimate that the future volatility is higher or lower in the near term than the longer term. If the market's estimates of implied volatility for the front-month call should rise while the back-month implied volatility estimate should fall, it is possible for the trader who is short front-month options and long back-month options to suffer losses in this market situation.

The time kappa/vega risk for the short front-month/long back-month call spread from the previous section is shown in Figure 6.1. Time kappa/vega is unimodally negative, larger in the back-month spreads and growing smaller in the front-month spreads. At its maximum, time kappa/vega risk is about 16 cents per spread but even 30 days later it remains above 10 cents.

While 16 cents may not seem like a large risk, remember that in many futures options markets this 16 cents may represent $80 (0.16 × $500) in real dollar terms if one whole futures point = $500. Even though $80 may seem relatively small for one time spread, many option spreads are margined only in the hundreds of dollars, and $80 may be a significant percentage of that margin. Time kappa/vega is a serious option risk and is quite different from the kappa/vega risk of the total position, which indeed may be somewhat neutral. The time kappa/vega risks of the short front/ long back spread resemble those of the kappa/vega of the short put, short call, and short straddle, which we have seen are unlimited-risk positions.

In option calendar markets, nearer options are generally priced with higher implied levels than back-month options. This feature may be called the *normal backwardation of implied levels,* although the degree of backwardation may vary considerably (Figure 6.2). In futures option markets, the higher implied volatility for front-month options is partially justified by the generally greater actual volatility in front- over back-month futures.

Nevertheless, the near-month implied level occasionally may fall lower than the back-month level in an implied volatility contango. Near-month implied levels in particular may fall lower than back-month levels as expiration nears, as heavy short premium selling by the public takes place, or as long seasonal holidays approach when light trading is expected.

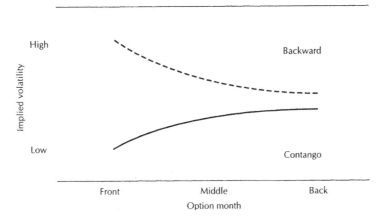

Figure 6.2 Implied volatility contango and backwardation of futures options.

Although time futures basis delta risk is not a serious or un-limited risk when properly hedged, the same is not necessarily true of time kappa/vega risk. The extent of backwardation in op-tion implied volatilities cannot be fixed in advance and is theo-retically unlimited (Figure 6.2). Futures options normally trade with implied volatility time spreads of only one or two points but may sometimes go out to 10 or more points, as happened in recent disorders in the stock and bond markets in 1987 and 1989.

Even if one assumes that an upward boundary of 10 or 20 points exists in the backwardation or contango of implied lev-els, a position with 1000 time spread contracts that experiences a kappa/vega risk of 16 cents per spread (or $80 in real dollars) will suffer an $800,000 loss in a 10-point move in implied backward-ation levels. A 10- or 20-point adverse move in the time implied volatility spreads may quickly send an option trader to the bottom of the sea if he or she is not careful. Although this may not happen often, it need only happen once to end an option business.

Time strategies differ significantly in their time kappa/vega risk. Some carry large negative time kappa/vega risk, and others do not. As we noted, the short front-month/long back-month option time strategy carries negative time kappa/vega risk. Theoretically, there are 400 distinctly different two-legged time spread strategies (20 single-month positions squared). It is beyond the scope of this text to present a classification of the limits of time kappa/vega for all these strategies. Nevertheless, for those strategies that carry large time kappa/vega risk, there is no expedient way to use futures to offset this risk, as is done to hedge time delta risk. Time kappa/vega risk is inherent in any option time spread and can only be hedged, if at all, by other option time spreads.

LIMITED AND UNLIMITED TIME RISK

The characterization of time spread positions as having limited or unlimited risk must be based on time delta and time kappa/vega risk evaluation, not single-month delta or kappa/vega risk. Unlike the bull or bear vertical spreads of a single month, which have a finite basis of gain/loss, many option time spreads do not have a basis limit to the losses sustainable in the event of the unexpected futures spread price or implied volatility change. Thus, the two-legged time spread is potentially an unlimited risk strategy if proper care is not taken.

As we have already discussed, futures options traders may successfully manage futures basis risk by hedging delta in each month with an offsetting futures delta position in that month. That is, the time option spread is crossed with a time futures spread, thus making each month delta neutral separately. While this procedure works tolerably well as a short-term hedge against time delta risk, it leaves unaffected time kappa/vega risk, which may remain potentially catastrophic.

Nothing says the short (front) month implieds must trade at parity for the long (back) month implieds as noted in the previous section. In the extreme case, front-month implieds may trade at two to three times the back-month implieds, representing an implied backwardation. In this case, a short front-month/long back-month position could suffer losses as great as if it had not been long back-month kappa/vega at all.

Assume, for example, that at a time when the front and back months are each trading at a 15 implied volatility level a trader shorts the front and buys the back for kappa/vega risk parity. Subsequently, the front-month implied rises to 30 while the back month rises only to 20. The loss of 15 implied volatility points in the front month is only compensated by a profit of 5 implied volatility points in the back month, for a net loss of 10 kappa/vega points.

The potential for a loss of 10 kappa/vega points is a serious financial risk. Furthermore, the risk is potentially unlimited, for the ratio of the short-month implied to the back-month implied may increase without limit. If the front-month implied moves from 15 to 60 and the back-month implied moves from 15 to only 25, then the spread will have moved 35 kappa/vega points against the trader—clearly a catastrophic loss.

It may be possible to compensate for this unlimited time kappa/vega risk on one leg by going long a greater kappa/vega in the back month relative to the short kappa/vega risk of the front month. Based on the kappa/vega spread possibilities of the preceding two paragraphs, a trader wishing to hold a short front-month/long back-month position should consider holding a short-to-long kappa/vega ratio of at least 1:3 to feel safe from an implied volatility blowout in the front month. A trader holding this position could see front implied levels go from 15 to 45, while back levels go only from 15 to 25 and would still not lose money.

While heavy weighting of back-month to front-month kappa/vega will protect the trader to some extent from an implied volatility blowout, it also leaves the trader heavily long kappa/vega overall. Should implied volatility levels decrease at the same absolute level for both front and back months, the short front/long back strategy, back-weighted, will suffer a severe loss.

In other words, by attempting to hedge against the possibility of an implied front-month blowout, a trader is exposed to a large single-month kappa/vega risk in the back month. Neither the parity kappa/vega two-legged strategy nor the back-weighted kappa/vega strategy is able to avoid severe and unlimited kappa/vega risk. Generally, therefore, the short front-month/long back-month horizontal time spread strategy is not strongly recommended.

A short front-month against a long back-month time spread will not be protected from a blowout in the short month implied ratios against the long month. Since this *horizontal* or *diagonal time spread* is often recommended as a safe strategy, a conservative trader will want to know that this statement is not necessarily so. A blowout in time implied volatility spreads could be (and has been) the downfall of many option traders. For this reason, the two-legged time spread strategy is not recommended where either leg is short kappa/vega as a single-month position.

However, not all two-legged time spreads are catastrophically risk-exposed—only those with short time kappa/vega risk. The only way to ensure that a time spread is hedged with respect to time kappa/vega risk is to hold limited kappa/vega risk positions for each time leg separately, as with time delta risk. For a time spread to be adequately hedged against time kappa/vega risk, each leg of the time spread must be a limited-risk option position. To be long two straddles, one in a front month and and one in a back month, is a limited time kappa/vega risk position, but a long/short time straddle position is not.

To determine whether a particular total carryover position is subject to unlimited time spread risk it is necessary to perform risk analysis on each calendar month position separately. In a two- or three-legged horizontal spread, if any single leg of the position is exposed to unlimited delta or kappa/vega risk, then the total position is probably so exposed, whether the kappa/vega offsets are parity or weighted in other months.

Hedging for time kappa/vega risk will considerably reduce the number of time spread strategies that a prudent trader will use. While there are 400 possible two-legged time spreads, there are fewer than 100 that have limited-risk exposure. These positions will be reconsidered in Chapter 7.

TIME BUTTERFLIES

Time spreading to a third leg may alter two-legged time delta and kappa/vega risks considerably. Time delta risk would initially increase owing to the exposure to a second futures time spread; but this change could be managed by doing offsetting futures hedges at the same time as in the two-legged time futures hedge. The nature of the time kappa/vega risk in a three-legged option strategy is more complex, however, and less frequently studied.

In a three-legged time spread probably the safest way to avoid the unlimited risk of the short two-legged time spread strategy is to bracket a short middle-month position with a long front- and back-month position. The latter strategy can neutralize the unlimited risk of the two-legged strategy if certain assumptions are fulfilled. If implied volatility time spreads trade in a semilinear or smoothly curved backwardation or contango, then this two-long, one-short month strategy may work successfully to limit risk, since the mean of the front and back implied levels may be set to equal the middle month level whether the implied time spread moves in contango or backwardation.

Unlike a two-legged short time spread, a three-legged long time spread may limit catastrophic time kappa/vega risk under certain market conditions or assumptions. However, traders should be aware that these conditions (semilinear implied contango or backwardation) cannot be assured. If the implied volatility spreads between the front, middle and back diverge from semilinearity in a significant way, the long kappa/vega three-legged strategy may become exposed to severe or potentially unlimited risk.

Such a split in implied contango/backwardation across cycles would be unusual but not impossible. There is no empirical or logical necessity that the implied levels of the middle month's position will approximate the mean of the front- and back-month position implied levels.

For example, consider the situation of a front old-crop month, back new-crop month, and a middle transition month characteristic of many seasonal agricultural options. Even when there is normal implied backwardation in the intracrop months, the intercrop spreads diverge according to fundamental considerations for kappa/vega that depend upon crop supply-and-demand seasonality. For seasonal crop options, it would be possible for the implied volatility spread to be in backwardation for the old-crop cycle, but in contango for the transition and new-crop months.

In short, trying to neutralize time implied volatility risk with different crop year options is a poor hedge. Should all months move against the long time kappa/vega butterfly trader simultaneously, the trader may suffer severe and possibly unlimited losses. Although nonseasonal commodities and financial option markets are not usually subject to violations of the assumption of the semilinearity of implied time spread, this also need not be the case. In the U.S. Treasury bond market, for example, refunding schedules may act to impose a seasonality in supply and demand not unlike seasonal commodities. These could act to produce irregular implied volatility time spreads.

Another disadvantage of a time butterfly strategy is that, as the front-month expires and the middle month becomes the front-month, the trader will be left with a short front-month/long back-month kappa/vega position, which we have already seen is a poor risk strategy. Since time butterflies turn into two-legged short time spreads over time, the long kappa/vega time butterfly strategy would require repetitive rollovers of position after each expiration, a time-consuming, expensive, and sometimes difficult task to do in all markets, given the irregular flow of broker orders.

Nevertheless, if the rollover of time butterflies can be accomplished successfully (and without compromising intercrop seasonality), these strategies may be prudent. Moreover, it is possible to use time butterfly strategies if the same principle is followed for prudently trading two-legged time spreads—that is, hold each leg of the spread as a limited-risk position separately. If kappa/vega risk is independently spread by month, then time kappa/vega risk is effectively neutralized. Several different multileg time strategies that have less risk than the short time strategies will be considered further when discussing optimum strategies for market makers in Chapter 7.

7

On Strategy

INTRODUCTION

If synthetic trading may earn a good income and is the most secure and risk-free of any option strategy, why would a market maker attempt to trade in any other way? Probably the chief reason for trading nonsynthetically is that it is not always possible to trade synthetics in all markets at all times. More trading generally occurs in out-of-the-money strike options than in the corresponding in-the-money strike options. Thus, a trader is able to buy or sell an out-of-the-money call but finds there is virtually no open interest in the corresponding in-the-money strike put with which to complete a synthetic trade.

Even with at-the-money options in which both strike pairs trade more regularly, there may be times when both strike sides of a near- or at-the-money option either will not trade at all or will not trade in a manner that permits the market maker to effect a favorable synthetic trade. Low-volume option markets in particular will often fall into the latter category, although high-volume markets may offer a niche for synthetic-only traders.

For these reasons, a market maker willing to trade synthetically only will often find that many markets are simply unavailable, resulting in a loss of potential income. Thus, to trade more actively—indeed, to make a market regularly in most strikes at all times—a market maker must frequently trade nonsynthetically in order to trade at all.

For a market maker, trading nonsynthetically carries more risk. If a market maker's nonsynthetic carryover position loses money, then the income earned market making may be wiped out. Market makers must perforce pay attention to nonsynthetic trading strategies, the risks they pose, and how to adjust and hedge positions.

When a market maker is not trading synthetically, the first decision he or she must make is to choose a strategy. There are about 20 basic single-month strategies and literally hundreds of possible time spread positions. Although earning the liquidity function profit of the bid/asked spread remains the overall goal of market making, what carryover position will be most appropriate? The ideal carryover strategy would (1) neither gain nor lose (especially lose) money over the long run, (2) allow the trader to keep net scalping profits, and (3) have a risk that minimizes bankruptcy and maximizes large payoff possibilities. Is there an optimum nonsynthetic carryover strategy for market making, and can it be executed?

If options truly have a fair value at trade prices, then theoretically the strategy used will make no difference whatsoever in profitability in the long run, since this is the definition of fair value. In other words, no option strategy is likely to have any different long-term payout than any other. But taking this theory at face value is to disregard preferences for risk. While either side of a futures or asset contract trade may have equal risk, all option strategies are not equal when measured from the standpoint of catastrophic risk or risk of bankruptcy.

Prudent market makers and dealers generally prefer limited-risk option (LRO) strategies over unlimited-risk option (URO) strategies as a means to minimize the risk of bankruptcy or default. A trader or firm can always lose some of its capital and then earn it back, but a person who loses his or her entire capital is out of the game. Specifically rejected as too risky from this standpoint are almost all short-time premium (positive theta, negative gamma/kappa/vega) strategies and many of the popular time spread strategies outlined in the previous chapter. An LRO trader who avoids these strategies sleeps more soundly and enjoys the weekends more than a URO trader.

In addition to the advantage of limited risk, many LRO strategies offer the possibilities of large profits on occasion. The opposite of catastrophic loss is extraordinary profit, and of the two, large profit is better than loss. Even if a market maker just breaks even on the LRO strategy over the long run, he or she will still attain the primary goal of keeping the liquidity function profits, which is the same objective as trading synthetics in the first place. But which LRO strategy should one pursue, and under what market conditions? This chapter attempts some answers to these questions.

One major difference between LRO strategies is that some have a delta directional bias and others are delta-neutral. The first section of this chapter discusses how technical analysis with trend predictive models may result in inconsistent success and how delta-neutral strategies are preferred. A delta neutral strategy allows the trader to earn non-trend-biased liquidity function profits and represents the profit for market making as a business.

The single-month positions that fit the conditions of both limited risk and delta neutrality are these: the long straddle/strangle, the long and short butterfly, and the long wrangle. The advantages and disadvantages of each will be presented in a subsequent section. These positions can also be used together in a time spread, which will be discussed in subsequent sections. The final portions of this chapter will consider how changing market conditions (broker order flow, fence markets, high-volatility periods and expiration) affect and change strategy.

DELTA (Δ) NEUTRALITY

For prudent market makers who wish to hedge risk and not speculate, delta neutrality is an important strategic goal. Strategies with a delta directional bias primarily interest option speculators who have opinions about market direction, whether based on technical or fundamental factors. Although market price prediction is not antithetical to or necessarily incompatible with market-making strategy, it is extraneous to it and often is not done well, resulting in losses.

There are several reasons market makers may wish to be delta neutral. First, speculative or directional strategies require the expenditure of time and effort in developing a technical or fundamental forecasting model of some sort, whereas market making is already a full-time trading activity. Since market makers need not have any opinion about the market to earn an income, some may find this added time and effort burdensome, or even distracting from the business of market making, and prefer to be delta neutral. Second, not having to worry about the direction of the market can confer considerable peace of mind to a trader.

What if the additional time and effort spent in forecasting prices bring additional profit, despite the accompanying psychological stress? No doubt for some this will be true. If a trader is able to predict the market successfully, then he or she will earn some speculative profit.

Earning liquidity function profits and earning a speculative profit are not mutually exclusive and indeed are the best of both possible worlds. Probably most market makers at one time or another have taken some speculative position in options, and often feel the allure of doing so again. Whether one can consistently earn money trading speculatively, however, is a much-debated question. Certainly, the popular do-it-yourself books on speculating promise high returns, but the empirical evidence is more equivocal. There are two approaches to speculating: those based on fundamental analysis of supply and demand and those involving a technical analysis of trading.

Fundamental Analysis as a Trading Strategy

Fundamental analysis is usually the purview of large informed capital interests, which have the means and commercial contacts to analyze fundamental data more accurately than anyone else. The large amount of capital that these informed interests control can move the market price in the direction of expectations, at least over the short run. Speculation based on fundamental analysis, therefore, may be considered the domain of the large informed capital interests. By its character, successful fundamental analysis excludes the majority of small nonindustry speculators from participation, since they have neither large capital nor inside or informed industry information about supply and demand conditions.

Technical Analysis as a Trading Strategy

Technical analysis, which dates from the nineteenth century, was developed to offer the small uninformed speculator the possibility of detecting the trading of large informed capital pools (*smart money*) and thus doing the same. Technicians assume (probably correctly) that large capital is usually right about price direction. When smart money is accumulating, it is time to buy, and when smart money is liquidating or distributing to the public, it is time to sell.

Since large capital is thought to be on the other side of small (public) capital in the accumulation/distribution cycle, some speculators adopt a *contrarian* perspective: Do the opposite of what *the public* is perceived to be doing. When all public speculators have bought (or sold) at the bullish peaks (and bearish troughs) there is no money left to push the market, and prices will reverse—as smart money was betting.

In classical technical analysis such as is found in Edwards and Magee (1957), price alone is deceptive in trying to identify large informed money interests, since price is often used by large capital pools as a smoke screen to lure unwary traders into taking incorrect bullish or bearish positions. Properly done, technical analysis relies upon price as a speculative guide only in conjunction with volume analysis. Classical technical analysis is really volume analysis, since the hidden tracks of large informed speculators are left in the trail of the volume of trading activity.

For a classical technical trader, a *head and shoulders* price formation, for example, must be confirmed in volume analysis. Thus, early technica was synonymous with *tape reading,* that is, deciphering the individual price and volume transaction records. Modern technical analysis now uses price and volume data to suggest that it is still possible to earn consistent speculative profits. By identifying where smart money is trading against the public, technical traders try to do what smart money is doing, and ride on its coattails to profit.

As with any form of advertising, it is "caveat emptor" about the claims made for technical analysis. While some individual traders have demonstrated their ability to earn large fortunes speculating, at least for some periods of time, many of these same traders have ended up losing most if not all of their capital if they continued to trade. It is not widely known, for example, that one of the legendary technically oriented traders, Jesse Livermore, ended his life as a bankrupt suicide. Livermore made and lost several million-dollar stakes before giving up (Sarnoff, 1967).

Setting aside anecdotal evidence, however, studies have shown that most speculators are not right and do not make money on average over the long run (Teweles and Jones, 1987). Some studies show as few as one in four speculators earning money over many years, and other studies show less success than this. Speculation is indeed risky.

Although most speculators lose money, studies also show that some, mostly large, speculators may do well consistently for many years (Maddala and Yoo, 1990). Large speculators appear to make money although there are fewer money makers than money losers. If we ignore commercial hedging profits/losses, we see that the speculative profit of the small group of large traders in effect comes at the expense of the cumulative losses of the large majority of small speculative traders.

The evidence suggesting that the majority of traders consistently lose money at the expense of a smaller number of larger traders is consistent with the premises of technical analysis. What the evidence does not confirm, however, is whether the technical analysis method of trading is able to improve the success rate of most speculators. For example one popular technically oriented stock forecasting model (the "Wall Street Week" Elves) was dropped from that program after completely failing to anticipate either of the stock market crashes of 1987 or 1989. *The Hulber Digest,* which tracks the trading records of many of the most popular technical trading advisories, has shown that many, if not most, overstate the success of their speculative trading results and that few consistently make money in all types of markets. The few large public commodity funds, which usually use technically oriented trading strategies, also do not appear to do well consistently when tracked over long periods of time, confiming the poor results of technically oriented speculation (see *The Wall Street Journal,* Jan. 28, 1991). Although technical analysis promises great financial success, the record suggests that most speculators will not be successful if they are undercapitalized with inadequate information, whatever method they use.

Most speculators lose money over the long run, and small technically oriented traders are likely to be losers. Although there are some successful large speculators, the overall odds are against small speculators, which most market makers would be if they speculated. In light of this situation, delta-neutrality is the appropriate strategy. Whether futures prices go up or down, delta neutrality assures the market maker a profit.

Floor traders who have traded speculatively and then attempt to become market makers have to give up thinking in terms of market direction. Remember, the object of any successful trader is to make money, not to be proved right. Market direction is only a means to an end, not an end in itself.

Summary

Regardless of the added work, since empirical studies have shown that most speculators are wrong and lose money, speculating in delta-directional strategies will often be a waste of time and money. For these reasons, risk-averse market makers will want to avoid speculative strategies generally, even if they have limited risk, and remain delta neutral. Of course, this rule is observed universally in the breach by taking *shots* once in a while, and seasoned market judgment may also recommend a non–delta-neutral strategy from time to time, provided the extra risks are understood.

CORE STRATEGY

Since different market participants may have different overall strategic goals, there is no such thing as the optimum option position for all risk tastes. For market makers qua dealers only, however, there will be a preference for limited nonspeculative (delta-neutral) risk strategies. Aside from synthetics, there are only four single-month positions that fit this limited-risk, delta-neutral (LRO–DN) profile: the long straddle/strangle, the long and short butterfly/condor, and the long wrangle. Each of these strategies will be reviewed and considered for relative advantages or disadvantages. The reader may wish to review the profit/loss and risk profiles of option positions in the Appendix to Chapter 4. Generally, the long butterfly/condor and long wrangle strategies are preferable to the short butterfly/condor and long straddle/strangle strategies for single-month positions. Time strategy will be considered in the next section.

Long Straddle/Strangle

The long straddle is an LRO–DN strategy that earns money in the event of wide futures price swings or increases in implied volatility (kappa/vega). Although a straddle will earn money with strong price moves in either direction, one can also make money with the long straddle by trading futures against the trend on large price-swing days. Since the straddle gets longer delta as futures prices rise and shorter delta as they fall, large swing days will earn profit, especially if adjustments are made at price turning points intraday. This trading strategy is known as *trading gamma,* which will be discussed more fully in Chapter 8. A long straddle holder will also earn additional profits if implied volatility levels increase greatly. If a wide futures price move and an increase in implied levels occur simultaneously, the profits to a long straddle holder can be substantial.

Some traders hold a *long volatility* philosophy of option trading, which says the long straddle is the optimum strategy. Despite its advantages, however, the long straddle strategy suffers from some serious weaknesses. The chief disadvantages of the long straddle are the high cost in negative theta risk (time premium decay against the trader) and the risk that volatility will not increase and may even fall. In the worst case, the combination of both, futures prices do not move and implied levels fall. A market maker who is long kappa/vega will attempt to continue to earn liquidity function profits to offset losses from time decay or minor falls in implied volatility, but a trader cannot always accomplish this and may take temporary and possibly large losses.

Although the long straddle is a delta-neutral strategy, it is not really a kappa/vega neutral strategy, and its losses, although limited, can be quite high if kappa/vega moves in the wrong direction. In extreme cases a sharp drop in implied volatilities from relatively high levels may approach or exceed catastrophic risk from the short side. Of all the LRO–DN strategies, the long straddle strategy is the most exposed to catastrophic kappa/vega risk in certain (high-volatility) market conditions.

Aside from risk considerations, market makers rarely hold pure straddles for the simple reason that making a two-sided market means that one will almost always be long and short options at the same time. The long straddle/strangle is probably the least desirable LRO–DN strategy both theoretically and practically for an active market maker.

Long Butterfly/Condor

The long butterfly/condor is the only LRO–DN strategy that is positive theta, at least some of the time. By being short more time premium in the center options against long time premium on the

wings, the long butterfly is *short premium* and will earn some
time decay profits so long as the butterfly remains centered at the
futures price.

As we noted in Chapter 4, one of the risks associated with
being positive theta is being negative gamma and kappa/vega in
single-month positions. For the butterfly, however, the negative
kappa/vega risk is contained by the protection that the butterfly wings afford should futures prices move off center by a large
amount. Although the long butterfly is positive theta in the center, kappa/vega is neutralized at the price extremes. If the market
remains in a period of low volatility, a butterfly earns a small time
decay profit, without the catastrophic risk of the short straddle
strategy. Because of the costs of neutralizing kappa/vega, theta
is less positive than the short straddle, and thus less profit is
earned. The long butterfly/condor is really the only prudent short
time premium strategy and is sometimes termed a limited risk
credit spread.

Short/Butterfly Condor

In the short butterfly, the limited risks of the long butterfly are
inverted; that is, negative theta and positive kappa/vega if futures prices remain unchanged but positive theta and negative
kappa/vega if futures prices move sharply in either direction. To
lose money to time decay in quiet markets but have only limited
profits in volatile markets is not a desirable strategy, given the
actual volatility of asset or futures prices. In effect, the short but-
terfly/condor has all the disadvantages of the long straddle without
any of its real potential to earn catastrophic profits. Long butterfly
strategies are preferable to short butterflies.

Long Wrangle

The long wrangle is an LRO–DN strategy that resembles the long
straddle in attempting to profit from high real and implied volatilities but without the drawbacks of the long straddle/strangle with
high negative theta. In effect, the long wrangle attempts to neutralize the disadvantages of the long straddle but retain its long
volatility risk profile.

The long wrangle strategy essentially utilizes the credit from
the sale of center strike options to purchase a greater number of
out-of-the-money options. When done carefully, the long wrangle

position can usually be put on at a credit and, therefore, is a limited-risk credit spread. By being short time premium in a credit spread, the long wrangle has a low negative-to-neutral (and sometimes even positive) theta at the center strikes, much like a long butterfly.

Although neutral theta in the center, the long wrangle will maintain a positive gamma and kappa/vega in the wing strikes. By remaining long positive kappa/vega, the long wrangle strategy may permit a trader to gamma trade when necessary, and benefit from a large upward move in implied volatility if futures move in either direction. Although it is not possible to be positive theta, positive gamma, and positive kappa/vega at the same time in the same single-month position, it is possible to do this in the same position over a range of strikes, which is what the long wrangle does in its trimodality of risk. It is this trimodality that makes the long wrangle a very versatile LRO–DN position for single-month strategies and closely relates it to the favorable trimodal risk profile of the long butterfly.

Despite the advantages of long wrangles, however, as complex ratio spreads they are particularly sensitive to skew risk. Skew risk in the vertical spread implied volatilities will generally affect all the delta-neutral limited-risk strategies. The positive (or negative) skew in put and call strike slopes will make wing strikes more (or less) expensive relative to at-the-money strikes. For example, in establishing long butterfly/wrangle carryover positions, a market maker is sometimes selling lower volatility (center) options and buying higher implied volatility (wing) options. However, the effect of skew risk is generally not fatal to the viability of long ratio strategies, although it will be discussed again in Chapter 8.

Comparison of Single-Month LRO–DN Strategies

The optimum single-month option strategy would be exposed to limited delta, positive theta, and positive kappa/vega risks. Such an option position would earn a premium time decay profit while also earning profit on futures price swings. A theoretically perfect option position would earn a profit no matter what happens to real and implied volatility levels. Unfortunately, the theoretically perfect option position is impossible for single-month positions.

The two credit-spread LRO–DN strategies considered above—long butterfly and long wrangle—each have one advantage of the optimum position, and also one disadvantage, since it is never possible to be positive both theta and kappa/vega simultaneously in a single-month position. The butterfly attempts to maintain a slight positive theta in the center but incurs small losses on the wings. The wrangle attempts to participate in a positive kappa/vega stance on the wings, while neutralizing theta in the center.

Generally, the long butterfly/wrangle strategies are positive or neutral theta in the center and neutral or positive kappa/vega on the wings; that is, they are both trimodal in risk. Because of their trimodality of risk, the long butterfly and wrangle strategies are probably the most appropriate stances to assume if the actual probability of futures price change is semilog normal. The long butterfly and wrangle positions will be positive-to-neutral theta during 68 percent of the time that futures price change occurs around the mean price (that is, plus or minus one standard deviation). The rest of the time, these positions will become neutral-to-positive kappa/vega when futures prices blow out. In the financial markets the appropriateness of trimodal risk positions for actual market conditions is suggested by the deviations from log-normality of asset prices. These also represent a trimodal error curve (see Figure 2.5).

In summary, market makers have a preference for limited-risk non–price-speculative strategies, among which the long butterfly/condor and the long wrangle positions are generally the most favorable for single-month strategies. The long straddle/condor position is too kappa/vega risky as well as being impractical for an active market maker, while the long butterfly is preferable to the short butterfly because of the likely real risk. Market-making positions with trimodal risk profiles are consistent with the trimodality of the deviations from normal theory found in market data.

TIME SPREADING

Time spreading improves the core single-month limited-risk delta-neutral strategies. Disregarding the straddle, there are nine combinations of two-legged horizontal spreads between the short/long butterfly and long wrangle single-month positions only. Are any of these time spreads preferable to others?

As contracts move into front-month status (with less than a month to expiration), selling the center strike options short is often popular with large institutional, commercial, or speculative traders. Such naked short selling in the front month, whether commercially hedged or not, tries to capture the most time decay profit. This situation creates net selling from the public to market makers, who then may become much too long kappa/vega. The strategic goal of the front-month position, therefore, should be to minimize negative theta risk and, if possible, to be slightly positive theta. The long butterfly is the only LRO–DN strategy that allows a trader to do this, and for this reason a long butterfly position may normally be considered the prudent market-making strategy for the front-month leg of any time spread.

Likewise, there is no point in holding positive theta (*short premium*) positions in the back months, where theta risk is low and time premium decay minimal. Rather, it would be better to be positive kappa/vega and participate in a futures price blowout or implied explosion, which may generate catastrophic profits. For these reasons, the long wrangle strategy may be preferred for back-month positions.

If one combines these desirable single-month strategies, a limited risk delta-neutral time strategy emerges that holds a long butterfly in the front month and a long wrangle in the back month. An example of such a time position is illustrated in Figure 7.1 using a 30 to 60 day futures option time spread and its payoff at expiration, with futures basis at zero, interest rates at 10%, and implied volatility at 15%. The positions are constructed using the long butterfly and long wrangle in the appendix to Chapter 4.

At 30 days before front-month expiration, the payoff of this time position resembles a long straddle, but by front-month expiration resembles the payoff of a long wrangle, with its characteristic W shape and trimodal risk profile. Time kappa/vega is positive on both the put and call out-of-the money wings, but negative in the center strikes. Time delta is either neutral or even slightly positive in the center strikes, but negative on the out-of-the-money wings. Time delta is not a serious risk if it is properly hedged with offsetting futures spreads, but time kappa/vega risk must always be evaluated with concern. However, the trimodality of the time kappa/vega risk for a long wrangle must be considered limited. The maximum negative risk, about seven cents for a minimum 10-contract time spread of this nature, is not large and is less than half the maximum risk of the short front/long back strategy.

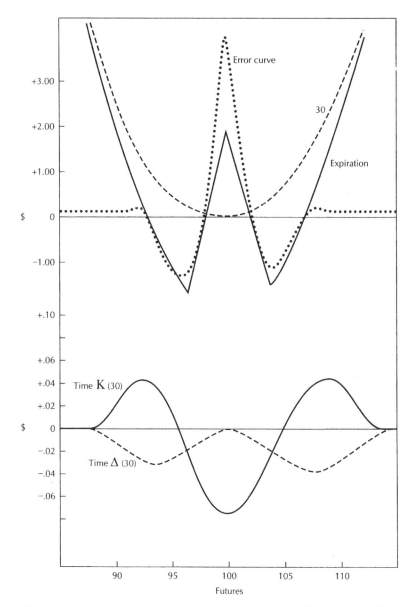

Figure 7.1 A time strategy. Error curve smoothed and fitted from Figure 2.5. Expiration refers to front-month option.

Moreover, the trimodality of risk allows this time position to become long time kappa/vega risk on either wing, which restricts risk while removing limits on profits. Generally, there is a long gamma/kappa/vega profile overall that may be actively gamma traded. The basic carryover position yields long delta on the upside and short delta on the downside, letting profits run. Should implied levels increase greatly in a futures price move, the time strategy will earn additional profits as a windfall. This combination of long gamma and long time kappa/vega gives the long butterfly/long wrangle time strategy its wallop.

Adding at least one back-month leg in a *time butterfly* would lend variation and some flexibility to the combinations of time spreads possible. With a time butterfly, it would be possible to carry for a limited time a short or negative kappa/vega single-month leg. From the standpoint of overall time strategy, however, nothing will change significantly from the risk/reward characteristics of the two-legged time spread if proper weighting has been achieved. Although the optimum strategies for all traders are likely to be somewhat different, depending upon market conditions and overall goals, the above position may be considered the basic workhorse of prudent time strategy for market makers.

Despite it advantages, there are some disadvantages to this time strategy that should be underscored. Skew risk in such a strategy becomes particularly important for any large ratio spread position, although it is in general still limited. Skew risk will be taken up again in Chapter 8.

Any long ratio spread will also be subject to catastrophic risk after an extremely large increase in implied levels, profitable as these may be. The only market condition that presents an unlimited risk to long ratio spreads is a high implied volatility level, which can fall precipitously. Although long ratio spread strategies may be the most profitable in the move from normal to high levels of volatility, they may also be among the most unprofitable in the move from high to normal volatility. This topic also will be reconsidered in Chapter 8.

Managing a time spread effectively over time requires attention to actual market conditions and to handling expiration dates and cycle rollovers successfully in order to maintain the time spread balance (a cycle rollover is a change in positions from one cycle to the next). A time spread is always changing as back months become front months, front months expire, and new months begin trading. A market maker is generally rolling over his or her time spreads constantly as one cycle expires and others begin; such rollovers may be made more or less difficult by market conditions. Issues related to expiration will be taken up later in this chapter.

Options usually do not trade in butterflies or wrangles outright. These complex strategies must be implemented separately by active trading, legging the component spreads in the total position. To some extent the actual supply and demand for options, by different strike and month, will determine how easy or difficult it is to maintain this core strategy. The supply and demand for options, which is essentially the net broker order flow, initiates most option trades.

BROKER ORDER FLOW AND OPEN INTEREST ANALYSIS

Any preferred strategy must be tested against market conditions and modified accordingly when conditions change. Among the most important market supply-and-demand conditions are broker order flows for options. Broker order flow becomes critically important in determining the ease of implementing complex option strategies.

Broker net order flow is simply the change in net balance of buying or selling by brokers of each option by strike and month. Since as much as 90 percent of all option trading is initiated by brokers and not market makers, the net balance of public orders is more important than the volume per se in ferreting out the supply-and-demand forces in the market. Open interest, the outstanding (existing) option contracts by cycle and strike, shows the result of broker order flows. Broker order flows and open interest will define fairly clearly a market's supply-and-demand structure.

Open interest is neither long nor short, since an open interest of one contract is always a buyer paired with a seller. As each day's trading is completed, the open interest is either subject to change, or not. Volume can raise or lower open interest, or leave it unchanged. If both sides of the trade are new initiators, then open interest increases. If one side is a new initiator and the other a liquidator, then open interest does not change. If both sides are liquidating existing positions, then the open interest declines. A market maker will want to know not only who initiated a trade, but how open interest was affected.

What is relevant in open interest is not only the size but also the side of the initiator of the original trade, and how these affect open interest change. Most trading in an option pit takes place between market makers and brokers, but it is the brokers who almost always initiate the order. Have brokers been net sellers or buyers of options? In which month and which strike? Are they putting on new positions or liquidating? Knowing who is buying or selling, and which market participants hold what option positions, can give a market maker an edge in knowing how to price option bid/offer spreads.

Broker order flow and open interest analysis are fairly easy, depending upon the size of the option pit (that is, the number of floor traders and brokers). The smaller the pit, the easier it is to follow order flows and open interest changes completely. In small pits (less than a dozen traders and brokers) determining order flow and open interest are almost an exact science if one is willing to do considerable work. In large pits of 40 or more traders, net broker order flow cannot be easily observed by any one trader in the pit, for large pits tend to fragment into smaller trading networks (Baker, 1984). Without an accurate gauge of net order flow, open interest changes will become less meaningful.

Nevertheless, a trader should learn to do this type of analysis as much as possible in any size pit. Following broker order flows in conjunction with open interest ideally gives an astute market maker information about the likely positions of most of the option trading market participants—that is, commercials or speculators (*the public*) and market makers (*the pit*)—what they are trying to do, and what strategy or pricing tactics are appropriate.

An option cycle begins up to a year or more before an expiration day. Since market open interest will be initiated by broker orders, the beginning of each option cycle starts with a broker net order flow (that is, the broker-initiated buying or selling of a specific contract or spread). For each cycle there are, as a practical matter, only five broker net order flow situations for single-month cycles. These are:

1. Equilibrium of supply and demand

2. Net buying of calls and puts (long volatility)

3. Net selling of calls and puts (short volatility)

4. Net buying of calls and selling of puts of different strikes (bull fence)

5. Net selling of calls and buying of puts of different strikes (bear fence)

An equilibrium in net broker order flow is probably the most favorable with respect to a market maker, since risk may be easily hedged with core strategy or outright synthetics. Less favorable are the other four market conditions, which require some strategy modification. Any long-volatility strategy will suffer some losses in the event of a persistent selling of options by the public, especially as expiration approaches. A short-volatility net broker order flow will limit the total position a market maker is able to carry. A long-volatility net broker order flow, however, may well bring unexpected profits to market-maker carryover positions; and this flow is favorable to core strategy up to a point. Long-volatility net order flows will eventually lead to high implied volatility prices, which may result occasionally in catastrophic profits for market-makers. (These topics will be further discussed later in this chapter.) Two other nonequilibrium conditions may be reflected in bull or bear fences in net order flow. Fences are used as an effective inventory hedge by commercials and often have the advantage of not incurring a debit since there is a sale and a purchase of options.

Consider the hypothetical beginning of an option cycle with heavy broker-initiated selling of out-of-the-money calls, light selling of at-the-money calls, heavy buying of at-the-money puts, and light selling of out-of-the-money puts (see Table 7.1). In this example, the predominant broker order flow is toward establishing a bearish fence for strikes above at-the-money, along with some other selling of out-of-the-money puts. Since the public, through

Table 7.1 Broker net order flows and open interest (single-month)

Strike	Calls	Puts	
High	1000[a] (heavy selling)		
At-the-money	100 (light selling)	1000[a] (heavy buying)	BEAR FENCE
Low		500 (light selling)	

[a] Indicates large open interest

brokers, is establishing a bearish fence, the pit will be doing the opposite side of the transaction as a bullish fence. Trading fences exclusively will present market makers with particular risk problems, which are discussed later in this chapter.

The broker net order flow may and does change over the course of an options life cycle, or even daily or hourly. Yet in many option pits, the trend of broker net order flow will often last for several weeks or months. It is important to identify these trends, for they are a key component in strategy.

The supply-and-demand forces for each option cycle may be followed by keeping a small notebook with the above market open interest conditions laid out, although with experience market makers may carry this information in their heads. An example of such record-keeping for broker order flows is presented in Table 7.2. From this schematic of current broker net order flows and open interest figures, it is possible to begin to estimate the entire public market position and trading activity and goals. In Table 7.2 one may see that brokers and the public are buying a bear fence in the back month, buying a bull fence in the middle month, and going short volatility in the front month. To interpret how these current broker order flows are related to existing positions it is necessary to follow the changes in open interest over several months.

At the beginning of each new option cycle, the broker order flow will quickly build up an initial open interest, since both sides of the trade (public and market makers) are establishing new positions.

Table 7.2 Broker order flows by contract month

Month	Front		Middle		Back	
Strike	Call	Put	Call	Put	Call	Put
High	H−		O		*L−	
At-the-money	*H−	*H−	*H+	O	*H−	L−
Low		*L−		H−		*H+

Key:
  H   Heavy activity
  L   Light activity
  O   Little trading (no broker bid/offer)
  −   Broker net selling
  +   Broker net buying
  *   High open interest

The predominant broker order flow will define the predominant open interest position directly in the back-month trading.

It is probably safest to begin any new position at the start of a cycle with long options or prudent spreads. If this proves difficult or untimely to execute to any size, then a net order flow is probably buying options and making them scarce. Correspondingly, if it becomes easy to buy options but difficult to sell them, then net order flow is selling options. Without equilibrium, a market maker will have some difficulty from the beginning in executing the legs or spreads necessary for prudent strategy.

When the transition is made from the back month to the middle month, one of two things may happen. Either broker order flow remains the same, or it changes to another of the five broker order flow types.

Let us consider the first case: Broker order flow in the middle month period remains the same as in the back month period. Under these circumstances open interest may continue to increase, or it may at some point become static. If open interest does not increase, any new trading is divided equally among those establishing new positions and those liquidating old ones. If open interest continues to increase, then accumulation will be occurring in both the back and the middle months. It is unlikely, however, that open interest would decline without a shift in broker order flow, since the pit and the public would not be changing sides; that is, liquidation could not occur without some change in broker order flow.

In the second case, a shift in broker order flow occurs. If open interest increases as a result, then new sections of the public and floor traders alike are establishing new positions. If open interest does not change, then the pit is probably shifting the risk of the different option positions held in open interest from one section of the public to another. If open interest falls, however, then the public has now begun to liquidate the positions it had already established.

In either case, market makers are looking for fundamental shifts in demand (accumulation) and supply (liquidation) for options, as expressed through the open interest and broker order flows. There must always be some accumulation in open interest at the beginning, but there need not be liquidation before expiration.

Over the life cycle of an option contract from back to front month, an option strike will first go through a stage of accumulation, as reflected by one of the five broker order flow conditions. These initial broker order flows may continue until expiration or change one or more times before then.

It is useful to have some strategic perspective on market structure. The general goal of safe market making is to establish a limited-risk option carryover position around which to make a market. Broker order flows, however, sometimes make this possible only to a limited extent; and market makers must think ahead to see what kinds of orders are most desirable or most likely to be possible.

Although the specific sequences that broker order flows may go through from beginning to end cannot be known in advance, a trader following market structure over time will have some idea where pressure on prices is coming from and how this pressure is effecting implied volatility change. A market maker should try to price competitively in the direction of the broker order flows over time, and look for options to trade strategically that will provide good spreads or time legs for limited-risk market-maker positions.

Generally a market maker will attempt to analyze open interest changes as a means of identifying the participants in the day's trading and interpreting what the future direction of supply and demand may be. By tallying an ongoing record of trades and open interest by strike, a market maker tries to ascertain the holders of the supply and demand for all option contracts. When distressed liquidation, overoptimistic buying or acute speculative buying by the public becomes apparent, a market maker will wish to adjust bid/offer spreads rapidly.

It is difficult to specify explicitly how the different combinations of broker net order flows in each of the option contract months and their changes will affect strategy in complex time spreads. Following broker order flows and strike open interest is sometimes an arduous and protracted affair in which perfection is impossible. The trader may expect some modest success in pits where he or she can generally observe most of the trading during the day. The chances for success are less in larger pits or under conditions of screen (upstairs) trading, where too much trading is going on simultaneously or is not available on a reporting system (for example, over-the-counter markets).

Nevertheless, following broker order flows as much as possible is a good trading strategy and may easily be worth the extra effort. The next two sections will deal with two important broker order flow market conditions: fences and high-volatility periods.

TRADING FENCES

In option markets it is not uncommon for the public to do explicit or implicit fences, forcing market makers to take the other side on balance. A fence-driven market, especially in smaller option markets, may make it harder for market makers to maintain delta neutrality or even to be positive or neutral kappa/vega. An option trader should be familiar with trading and adjusting option fences, since these may be the dominant trade in broker net order flow for periods of time.

There are two broker net order flow fences: a bear and a bull (Figure 7.2). A *bear fence* is a short call/long put and a *bull fence* is a long call/short put, where the options are of different strikes. Fence option strategies are commonly used by commercials who

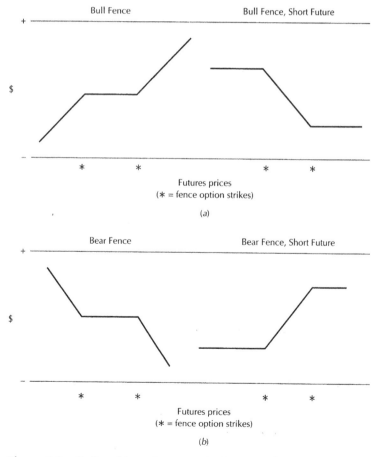

Figure 7.2 Bull and bear fence expiration payoff and with futures.

wish to hedge spot prices for one reason or another. For example, a commercial who is long inventory or futures will buy a bear fence in options for protection or hedge against spot inventory price declines. In this case, the bear fence with the long future or inventory will equal a vertical bull spread. Fences are particularly attractive for commercial hedgers since, if the cost of the option purchased is equal to or less than the cost of the option sold, the fence can be established without a debit other than basic margin.

Fences pose special problems to market makers since the short option wing of the fence is exposed to unlimited delta and kappa/vega risks. To be prudent, market makers must hedge both these risks, thus *closing the fence.* The key unhedged option in a fence is the short side option. Additional trades in futures, options, or some combination of both will neutralize the short side risk and close the fence.

Five ways to close the fence to unlimited risk exposure are discussed below, along with the disadvantages of each.

1. *Use futures to establish a vertical spread.* The simplest way to close a fence is to take a position in the assets market that is the opposite direction of the fence. Holders of bear fences will buy assets and bull fence holders will sell assets. The resulting position is either a bull or a bear vertical spread (which mirrors the opposite position of the commercial hedgers with inventory).

   Although *spreading the fence* will curtail the unlimited risk from the short option (by doing in effect a covered write), the resulting position will not be delta-neutral. Also, since only futures have been used to hedge the short option, there remains some (limited) risk of kappa/vega exposure. Although the total spread-adjusted fence will not be net short options, the option that is short will be of a different type from the long option and probably of a wide strike difference. If there is a wide implied volatility skew difference between the wings of the fence, a market maker will still be exposed to some possibly severe financial risk from kappa/vega risk. Because a futures/asset adjusted fence is not delta-neutral and has some kappa/vega risk, closing a fence with futures offsets is not the best response to these market conditions although it is acceptable if it is the only alternative possible, as sometimes it is.

2. *Synthesize the short option.* Synthesizing the short option, by buying the opposite side of the same strike and hedging with futures, will leave the trader with a simple long net option position. The trader will now hold a conversion or reversal at the strike of the short option, and the original long option of the fence will be held alone. Of course, if both strikes of the fence were synthesized (by doing the opposite side of the fence with another fence with opposite side options), a box would result, one of the lowest-risk option positions.

   Unfortunately, if there is a persistent broker order flow on one side of the fence, boxing the fence is rarely possible. Even synthesizing on the short side alone is not always possible.

3. *Buy different strike options on the short side of the fence and adjust with futures (step spreading/ratio spreading).* Buying more of the short side options of a different strike will effectively reduce the unlimited-risk wing of the fence by spreading. If a trader buys a higher strike option of the same type that is short, the resulting position will be a vertical step spread in the short direction and an open long position in the other direction. If a trader buys a lower strike option of the same type that is short, a ratio spread will be created in the direction of the original long option of the fence.

   However, if the broker net orders are persistently trading a particular fence, there may be few options of the short side available with which to create these favorable spreads and close the fence.

4. *Buy more of the long side options of different strike (convert to long ratio spread).* Buying more of the long side of the fence, and using futures to offset the short option side, can also close the fence. Unlike the other situations, when brokers are trading fences heavily, the long side option often may be obtained cheaply because brokers are attempting to leg the fence separately, or are willing to trade ratio spreads. If the fence can be closed by buying more of the long side options, the result will be a long ratio spread in the direction of the long options.

   As with spreading the fence using futures only, buying more of the long side options alone will leave the trader without any long options of the short side type for protection in the event of an upside blowout in the implied volatility skew. However, since the trader is now net long options, there is greater protection than if a fence were closed using futures alone. Also, by buying more of the long option side of the fence, a market maker may more easily obtain delta neutrality for the near future.

5. *Time spread.* Time spreading may also close the fence. However, offsetting a fence in one month with a position in another month exposes the total position to new time risks that must be considered, as seen in Chapter 6.

These are the main ways to close a fence, although other more complex spread or time trades may also work. Unfortunately, many ways of closing the spread have attendant difficulties. Using futures alone to spread the fence leaves the market maker exposed to some skew volatility risk, and a futures-adjusted fence also is not a delta-neutral position. Synthesizing the fence is, of course, the optimum from the standpoint of risk, but it is often impractical or impossible. Vertically spreading the short option side will also close the spread, but in case heavy broker net order flow is doing only one direction of the fence, getting long the short option side may prove difficult, especially in smaller, less liquid pits.

Buying more of the long side of the fence and adjusting with futures (going long a ratio spread) will often be most nearly optimum from the standpoint of risk, cost, and market conditions. By heavier weighting on the long option side, one can also neutralize delta over the short run. The disadvantage of this means of closing the fence is that the trader becomes excessively long kappa/vega on the long option side (as is most of the rest of the pit) and will not be delta-neutral near expiration. Nevertheless, this situation will be a limited risk that can be adjusted.

Time spreading, of course, may be used to close a single-month fence in different ways. A second fence in a different cycle could be used to close a fence in another month; if this time spread was a bull and bear fence, then the total risk of the position would be considerably reduced and would have the advantage of being delta neutral as well. Nevertheless, this spread position would eventually face the problem of rolling over or ending at expiration. The risk from holding fences in one month may also be offset by other time leg positions, a topic taken up in the tactics of time spreading (Chapter 8).

TRADING HIGH VOLATILITY

If one takes long periods of historical and implied volatility into account, the volatility of asset and futures markets separates into two groups: There are periods when the ranges in volatility are relatively normal, and there are periods when they are extremely high. For many commodity futures and options markets, the normal range (based on long-term historical averages) may be considered as anywhere from 10 to about 25. High ranges can be anywhere from 25 to the high 100s, and these appear suddenly, without warning from immediately preceding prices. Of course, each asset or futures option market has its own normal and high volatility ranges (for example, see Figure 7.3). High-volatility shocks rarely last more than a half year before normal long-term averages are restored. Normal ranges of historical and implied volatility are characteristic of market conditions about 75 to 80 percent of the time, with high volatility characterizing the rest of the time.

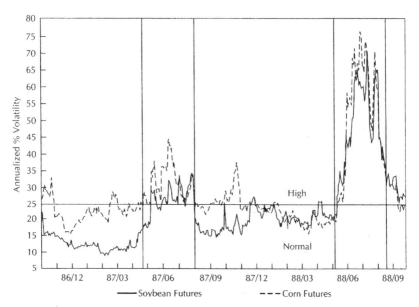

Figure 7.3 Implied volatilities of soybean and corn futures: Nearby series (October 1, 1986–September 30, 1988). (*Source:* Chicago Board of Trade, *Commodity Futures Professional,* January 1989.)

High-volatility periods offer the prospect of larger market-maker profits in several ways. For example, high trading volume often accompanies high-volatility periods, and the increased trading is good for normal business. Also, the higher volatility of the underlying asset will tend to widen the bid/asked spread in a dealer market, leading to a higher (potential) gross profit.

High-volatility periods also offer the promise of larger profits if the strategy has been designed—with a long gamma and kappa/vega risk stance—to maximize position profits at these times. Indeed, it is during periods of high volatility that the long kappa/vega time strategy comes into its own, and market makers may participate in very large profits. For the other traders who have assumed unlimited risks, times of high volatility bring great danger and risk of financial catastrophe.

Going into a high-volatility period, there are two main ways a trader derives profit from a long kappa/vega strategy: from the delta or gamma profits that are a result of widely fluctuating asset or futures prices; and from the potential for an increase in the implied volatility level.

In the first case, profits will accrue as asset prices move in one direction or another because the long kappa/vega strategy is also long gamma. Knowing if and when to take this profit, wholly or in part, is the essence of *gamma trading*. If the asset price continues to run strongly in one direction after the initial volatility shock, then very large profits will continue to be earned. Should asset prices move sharply backward in a reversal, these same profits can disappear rapidly. In a market of high volatility, frequent asset price reversals, and *whipsaws*, capturing profits may be easier if delta-neutrality is re-established more frequently.

A compromise tactic would probably take advantage of both ways to gamma trade and lock in some profits from any initial volatility shock price move. A long volatility position would want to lock in at least some profit from large asset price moves to be prudent, but still let some profits *run*.

In the second case, profit will result if implied volatility levels increase along with the change in asset volatility. Implied levels are likely to respond upward, even if only to reflect higher asset volatility, especially if the change was unexpected. However, if large sections of the market are caught holding short kappa/vega positions in the initial volatility shock, there may be a secondary shock in implied levels when a short squeeze develops among the negative kappa/vega traders who are weakly capitalized and vulnerable to exploding margin and clearinghouse requirements. In effect, a short squeeze will often develop after a sudden increase in historical volatility, which will then push option prices (and implied volatilities) even higher. Short covering negative kappa/vega traders will frequently push option prices (and volatilities) extraordinarily high, as few remain who are financially able (or willing) to sell options to those covering their short positions. An example of this short squeeze and implied volatility blowout took place during the stock market crash of 1987 when short out-of-the-money stock futures *calls* actually rose in price, reflecting implied volatility levels as high as 140 despite a 500-point drop in the Dow Jones Industrial Average!

Whether one is net long or short options ultimately determines whether one experiences catastrophic profits or losses in a move from normal to high real or implied volatility levels. If the long volatility strategy earns the most profit in high volatility periods, the negative kappa/vega strategy will often be financially devastated by high real or implied volatility. This situation is probably the most common cause of option trader blowouts. Even if a trader is short only $1,000 kappa/vega, he or she could suffer a $100,000 loss if implied volatility suddenly increased 100 points, as happened in 1987 and again in 1989. If one option trader's gain is another's loss, it is better to be on the side of the gainer in these normal- to high-volatility transitions, which is why prudent strategy remains neutral or positive kappa/vega during periods of normal implied volatility levels.

Despite the advantages of an initial long kappa/vega risk stance, some dangers that are inherent in this strategy must be understood and rectified when appropriate. A long kappa/vega position is best situated in a volatility explosion, but it is not necessarily the best situated once high volatility has peaked. Trading during periods of high volatility requires special attention to new and dangerous risks. It is one thing to make money on the increase in volatilities from 20 to 80, but another to give it all back, and more, as volatilities go from 80 to 20! Sooner or later high market prices and implied volatility levels will drop, sometimes even in the face of an extremely large futures price move; for example, the spike in crude oil implied volatilities on January 24, 1989, and January

16–17, 1991, which rose to an implied volatility level of 150 in one case, only to crash to 50 overnight, even with a large percentage drop in futures prices.

Like the wise gamma trader coping with an extraordinary rise in real volatility levels, the positive kappa/vega trader should lock in some (ultimately) large portion of profits by selling options and attempting to reduce the long kappa/vega exposure. A large positive kappa/vega will reward the trader with large profits in the transition to high-volatility periods, but once in a high-volatility period, a positive kappa/vega risk becomes catastrophically exposed and must be prudently lowered. It is during high-volatility periods that even a long kappa/vega trader may inadvertently suffer serious financial difficulties if he or she remains large positive kappa/vega too long. For this reason the volatility risk exposure of a market maker's carryover position should be hedged by selling options to achieve some degree of kappa/vega neutrality. These sales will lock in market-maker profits without further market risk.

Sometimes, when asset prices become more volatile, the implied volatility level of options may stay the same or even drop! There are several reasons why asset prices and option volatilities may not move in the same direction together. It is possible that the total market already holds low-risk offsetting positions and that there is no large group of short kappa/vega speculators caught short and needing to cover—possible, but not always likely. An inversion between market prices and implied volatility levels would also signal the market's opinion that the increase in market volatility is temporary and will soon collapse. For whatever reason, however, an implied volatility/market inversion in a high-volatility period is likely to be financially disastrous to a heavily long volatility strategy. Although such a strategy is low risk, it is not *no risk*; an inversion is perhaps the largest risk event that this strategy will experience. Long ratio or wrangle strategies will be particularly exposed to inversion risk since the ratio structure of the position risks going into a falling implied volatility period at the same time that the position gets longer volatility.

To offset the potential loss from the inversion of the implied levels, the long volatility strategy expects to earn profit from the gamma trading or the run in delta. It is possible that losses from a collapse in implied levels may be greater than the profits from gamma, in which case the position would show an overall loss.

Because implied volatility may drop in the event of an increase in asset price volatility, the long ratio volatility strategies are not without some major financial risk under some market conditions.

Consider a real situation, in which asset prices went from $40 to $20 in one month, a 50 percent drop, yet implied volatility dropped from 150 to 40 at the same time; this happened on the oil option market of the New York Mercantile Exchange in the first few months of 1991. Under such conditions a trader holding a long bear ratio put spread would have gained some gamma profit as prices slid 50 percent, but would also have suffered some losses due to the collapse of implied volatility. Indeed, it is not impossible that the losses on kappa/vega risk would be larger than the profits from the asset price move in this situation.

A condition in which sharply lower asset prices lead to a drop in implied levels may be more characteristic of commodity markets rather than other option markets. Sharply lower stock prices in 1987 and 1989, for example, were accompanied by sharply higher implied levels, proving profitable to the long ratio put holder.

Given these possibilities, prudent strategy will seek to understand the different market and implied volatility relations in the specific market being traded. A prudent strategy may attempt to weight the wings differently in a delta-neutral butterfly/wrangle position, in the direction of the appropriate price movement up or down, to take into account the possibility of an implied level inversion to high market asset price volatility.

As a final note, implied levels may temporarily trade at different levels from high real volatility if there is a limit restriction on futures price change in one day but not on option prices. In such a case, option implied levels based on limit futures prices will not accurately reflect true market conditions. For example, assume futures prices are at 100 and a constant option implied level of 10. If futures prices should make a limit move of 2 points to 102, and there are no price limits on options, then the formula for implied volatilities based on the limit price (102) will be inaccurate if options are reflecting a higher futures price. If implicit *as if* futures are trading at 104 instead of 102, then calls will be overvalued and puts undervalued using a 102 futures price in determining implied levels. In these market situations, true implied levels are likely to fall between the implied levels of puts and calls and would be the put and call average.

Conversely, with the average put and call implieds, one can compute *as if* futures prices based on option synthetic prices. For example, if after the limit move of futures from 100 to 102 the true implied level remained at 10 (despite calls settling at 12 and puts at 8), then market makers would immediately be able to determine the *as if* futures price based on postlimit market synthetic put/call prices.

Market makers will always know what the *as if* futures prices are, and even the contango or backwardation in the futures time spread, based on fair-value option sheets. With knowledge of *as if* prices, futures options market makers can continue to make market and trade options, provided they take care not to violate any of the risk prudence of the core strategies. Even if future prices have moved the limit, market makers can continue to trade gamma using options trades. With care, the potential profits remain large.

EXPIRATION

Incorporating the inevitability of expiration into a trading strategy requires skillful management of changing option risk. As middle-month positions turn into front- and near-expiration-month positions, kappa/vega risk is greatly diminishing, but gamma and theta risks are growing rapidly. The drift in delta may become quite severe in nonsymmetrical positions as standard deviation shrinks on a daily basis. At this time a trader often must pay special attention to position adjustment if he or she is not holding a synthetic position.

For the long butterfly, delta adjustment near expiration is somewhat like trying to balance a ball on the end of a pointed stick. The large negative gamma means that a trader will be buying or selling futures, or delta, in the direction of the market more frequently, and consequently suffering more frequent whipsaw losses. The compensation is higher positive theta and time decay profits near expiration, but it often seems to the short premium trader that the time decay profits do not cover the gamma adjustment losses. If a trader minimizes gamma adjustment to avoid whipsaw losses, the market may seem to choose that very time to make a big trend move in one direction or the other.

For the long straddle or wrangle trader, the situation is just the opposite. Positive gamma means that no adjustment is required in the event of a futures price move, and consequently there is no risk of whipsaw losses. But the long extrinsic value of the position is decreasing rapidly. If futures do not move in price, the long straddle/wrangle trader may suffer net losses despite gamma trading if negative theta becomes greater.

It is also true that many positions carried near to expiration begin to display quirky risk features if the distance between the component strikes is too wide. As noted previously, a long butterfly is considered a limited-risk option position because the short center straddle is theoretically risk-hedged by the long strangle on the wings. This protection, however, will work only if the strike spreads are close enough in standard deviations to be meaningful. Near to expiration, if the wings are several standard deviation points (say, five or six) away from the center strikes, then scant protection may be provided in the event of a large futures price move. Long wrangles will also begin to take on the risk profile of short straddles near expiration if the out-of-the-money strikes are too many standard deviations away from the center and futures remain in the center. Generally, a large option position will begin to shrink its risk profile to that of the options with strikes closest to where futures prices are trading. This change may alter the real dollar risk to the position.

To avoid many of these problems of severe risk drift and quirkiness, an option trader should run hypothetical at-expiration profit-and-loss risk profiles of large positions by month beginning several months before expiration. Doing so will allow a preview of special or large expiration risks that a trader may wish to correct before expiration arrives.

For traders with long kappa/vega positions in the back and middle months, the approach of front-month status will require some changes in strategy. Generally, a trader does not want to go into front-month status too long kappa/vega, in the event that short premium sellers may force down prices to expiration. Yet the limited-risk trader does not wish to go short kappa/vega and join the short premium sellers either. From day 45 to about day 30, therefore, it is advisable to adjust to only moderately long kappa/vega. During this time a trader should look for spreads that will reduce quirky risk features of option positions being held.

When the front month becomes one month or less, a trader may wish to consider *synthesizing* as many spreads as possible into conversions or reversals. Synthesizing an option position in effect "lands" a position safely at expiration with the minimum amount of risk and is recommended for risk-averse market makers. Generally, large open or nonsynthetic option positions should not be carried into the expiration week or day if it is possible to avoid them.

In Chapter 5 we noted that even synthesized option positions will carry expiration risks if assets or futures prices are trading at or near the synthetic strikes at the cycle close. This is known as *pin risk*. That is, the trader risks being *pinned* to the strike on the short option side. As a result, the trader suffers overnight uncertainty about whether he or she will be exercised against and about how many futures to carry overnight. An incorrect judgment about futures carryover may mean that the trader is not delta neutral on the morning opening after exercise and will suffer large windfall losses (or profits).

For these reasons, a market in trading at-the-money strike synthetics sometimes will develop at or near expiration as traders attempt to avoid pin risk. Traders holding synthetics will try if possible to liquidate with other traders holding the opposite side of the synthetic (conversion or reversal). These trades are usually done at fair value with no profit for either trader. Since the pit has often been on the same side taking public orders, however, liquidating synthetics without loss is not always possible except in limited instances. When the pit is mostly on one side of a synthetic, at-the-money synthetics will trade at a slight premium for the added expiration risk.

It is lore among floor option traders that futures prices tend to gravitate at expiration to the option strike with the largest open interest. Of course, it is always possible that this is the perception of all people who fear the outcome for themselves if they happen to be holding part of that largest open interest strike. As we shall see, there may be some market justification for this popular belief.

By no means all option traders will be holding synthetics at the near-expiration strike. Since we have already seen that the gamma of a near-strike option will be greatly increased near expiration, in practice an option trader who wishes to remain delta-neutral will be making frequent adjustments. Whenever futures prices trade above or below the strike in question, however, the adjustments required for an at-the-money option at expiration will be reversed. For example, a short call holder will attempt to buy futures if futures prices rise above the strike and sell futures if they drop below the strike. Of course, the long call holders will be attempting to do the opposite to remain delta-neutral. Thus, for the holders of non-synthetic at-the-money options near expiration, futures prices rising above or falling below the at-the-money strike will produce a flurry of trading adjustments that will send futures prices gyrating above and below the at-the-money strike. This phenomenon grows especially noticeable on the very last day of option trading before expiration.

If this explanation is a fair description of the adjustments that many traders undertake near expiration, then the strike with the largest open interest will also have the largest number of traders making adjustments when futures are above or below this strike and, thus, the largest impact on futures prices at this time. It is quite possible, therefore, that the strike with the largest open interest near expiration will be drawing futures prices up or down to this strike as part of the adjustment strategies peculiar to expiration. Futures prices may gravitate toward the largest open interest strike for these reasons, confirming market perceptions.

Expiration risk also includes the risk of early exercise or assignment of options. For underlying asset markets where forward price is not always taken into account in the option itself (unlike futures options and markets), the present value of future value or forward price must be implicitly derived before determining the pre-expiration exercise value of an American option. In the case of futures options, however, the desirability of early exercise to the long option holder may directly be determined and will be considered for illustration.

Generally, a long futures option should be exercised when the cost of carry becomes equal to or greater than the value of the corresponding strike pair option. If a trader exercises when the cost of carry is less than the value of the strike pair option, then he or she would give the value of the difference to the short option assignee as a windfall profit. If a trader does not exercise a long option when its cost of carry becomes greater than the value of the strike pair option, then the nonexerciser has also given a profit to the short option holder that equals this difference.

The following simplified example may make this clear. Assume the following prices and values with 30 days to expiration:

$$
\begin{aligned}
\text{Futures price} &= 100 \\
\text{90 put} &= 0.20 \\
\text{Interest} &= 12 \text{ percent per annum}
\end{aligned}
$$

From the synthetic parity formula, the fair value of the 90 call in the above example would equal intrinsic value (10.00) plus the value of the 90 put (0.20), discounted by the cost of carry for one month. The cost of carry for an option synthetically valued at 10.20 would be 0.102 for one month. Since the cost of carry is less than the value of the corresponding strike pair put, the long 90 call holder would not wish to exercise. If the market value of the 90 put were 0.05 rather than 0.20, however, then the long call holder would wish to exercise to avoid excess costs of carry.

It may be seen from the foregoing that the risk of early exercise or assignment to the short futures option holder is not large. If the long option holder exercises too early—before the cost of carry is above the value of the strike pair option—then the short option trader in effect gains the long option at a discount. If the long option holder fails to exercise after the cost of carry is above the strike pair option, then the short option trader is earning a premium interest on his or her net credit position.

Early exercise is not really much of a risk, but in fact, will almost always work to the market maker's advantage in futures options markets. In the cash option market, early exercise may present a somewhat different situation, which must be examined more carefully based on the cost of carry of the underlying financial asset and its forward price.

8

Market-Making Tactics

INTRODUCTION

The simple mechanics of "giving a market" are not difficult to learn. A market maker will have access to *fair value sheets*, which are printed daily, that list the BSM fair value of different options based on current market implied volatilities at different hypothetical futures prices. Fair-value sheets are printed daily or even intra-day by option software services (see Appendix) or by market makers themselves on private option software. A fair value sheet for calls will give information similar to that in Table 8.1, with the delta of the option listed in parentheses. In this example, the March expiration is 60 days away and the May 120 days, with implied volatilities at 15 for all options (a flat call skew).

If the futures price, for example, is trading at 100, then the March 100 call would have a fair value of 2.40 and the 105 call would be valued at 0.75, when market implied volatilities are at 15. By bidding somewhat below this value and offering somewhat above this value, a market maker gives his or her market. For example, a market maker might typically give "30, at 50" for a price quotation on the March 100 call when March futures are at 100, that is, 2.30 bid, offered at 2.50. If the futures price rose to 101 the market on the March 100 call would be "85, at 05," that is, 2.85 bid, offered at 3.05. (Generally, quotes are given in dollars and cents for a single option, as in $2.50 bid for the 100 call. The

Table 8.1 Hypothetical fair values for March and May calls

Futures Price[a]	March		May	
	100	105	100	105
101.00	2.95	1.00	3.90	1.85
100.50	2.65	.85	3.60	1.70
100.00	2.40(.50)[b]	.75(.22)	3.35(.50)	1.55(.30)

[a] See Table 5.3 for complete prices
[b] Value of delta in parentheses

actual amount of the contract is always considerably more than this, of course, depending on the value of the the contract. Cents are sometimes referred to as "ticks" or "points" and dollars as "whole points," although there is variation in each option market.)

The width of the bid/offer spread is usually a function of the overall volume of options traded and the number of market makers competing. Generally, the larger the volume and the greater the number of market makers, the smaller the bid/offer spread. Also, within any specific pit, the bid/offer spread will usually be narrower in the front months and wider in the back months, which reflects the different costs of doing futures hedges in more or less active futures months. If a trade is completed at the market maker's price, then the market maker will expect to earn the difference between the bid/offer price and fair value as profit.

If requested to do so by brokers, market makers may also give quotes by size for the amounts at bid and offer price, where one contract equals one "lot." For example, if the market maker is 2.30 bid for 20 lots, with 50 lots offered at 2.50, the quote may be made as "2.30 at 2.50, 20 by 50." If size is not quoted, a market maker is required to trade at least one lot at his quoted prices, but will usually be ready to trade much more than this to retain the interest (and respect) of brokers. If this transaction represented the total of all the skills needed to make a market in options, then computers could probably replace individuals in the pit completely. However, giving a market on an option is only one (small) step in successful market making.

By now, one should understand from this text that the real skill of market making comes in maintaining the appropriate delta-

neutral limited-risk option carryover positions. Without a risk- defined strategy the market maker will risk losing not only the liquidity function profit but also his or her entire capital. A market maker,
therefore, must earn single trade profits, but do so within an overall risk-controlled strategy with adequate tactics. Previous chapters
have discussed strategy, while this chapter considers tactics.

Having established a delta-neutral limited-risk position of
some size, a market maker can give a market on both sides for all
strikes for at least some quantity. This allows the market maker
to earn a liquidity function profit without being too concerned over
the short term about market price or volatility direction.

Nevertheless, the accumulation of market-making trades will
mean at some point that the total position must be readjusted
to maintain the original or desired optimum carryover position. A
short straddle cannot be sold in quantity or continually without at
some point becoming exposed to too much kappa/vega risk. Some
form of spread trading or wing adjustment must be made. Also,
asset or futures price movements will mean that the delta neutrality of most option positions will be changing to positive or negative
and must be readjusted to neutrality. Thus, a market maker will
be looking to make frequent delta or kappa/vega risk adjustments
to the carryover position. The easiest way to do this is an option
spread.

MAKING A SPREAD MARKET

In initiating a position from the start and attempting to maintain one of the limited-risk positions on carryover, one must always begin by buying options and being long some volatility. This
statement is self-evident in the case of the long straddle (which
a trader only buys), but is also true for the separate initiation of
a long butterfly or wrangle position. The long butterfly or long
wrangle is always initiated by buying the straddle/strangle first,
before selling a strangle/straddle against it.

Generally, these are the axioms that a prudent option trader
will always follow: Go long before going short, and always remain
net long more options than those short. A market maker should
only sell what he or she already owns or is risk-hedged against.

Short options need not be hedged only with other options, of
course. Futures contracts are often used as delta hedges against

option positions. But from the standpoint of catastrophic risk, delta hedging is inadequate and will fail over the long run if it is used exclusively against short positions. The basis of all successful risk hedging is both delta and kappa/vega hedging. Since the only way to hedge an option's kappa/vega is with another option, all effective risk hedging must involve option spread trading. Having achieved a comfortable equilibrium with a limited-risk position, a trader will always be looking to do more spread trades, either outright, or separately.

The first things a market maker will look for in the pit at the opening of trading are (1) the prices at which options are trading and (2) the options that have changed from the implied volatility settlements of the previous day. This information will indicate whether the market maker's own fair-value sheets, based on the settlements of the previous day, need to be adjusted up or down before giving markets. This analysis need not involve printing new sheets (which would be inconvenient after trading has started); simply raising or lowering bids or offers to the appropriate implied volatility level is appropriate. As an added convenience, some fair-value software will even print fair-value sheets with multiple levels of fair values for different implied levels.

After the initial spurt of market orders and limit orders has traded, there will often exist declared broker orders that did not trade. These are then publicly *posted* on the option board. Boards are typically computer or electronic screens either on the exchange floor or on off-floor terminals. A typical option board might look like Table 8.2 after the opening call. This board indicates a broker's order of 2.65 bid and a market-maker or broker offer of 2.95 on the 100 call. If the futures price remains trading at 100 then the 2.65 bid is above the 2.40 fair value of the call (from Table 8.1) when implieds are at 15. In fact,

Table 8.2 Option board

	March	
95 call		
100 call	2.65 B	2.95 A
105 call		0.80 A

the 2.65 broker bid represents a 15 implied if futures prices were trading at 100.50, not 100. The market-maker offer, however, is made at a hypothetical futures price of 101, an even higher implied volatility than the broker bid. Temporarily, the market is bidding for a higher implied volatility than settlement volatility on the 100 call without finding any market makers willing to sell.

In this situation, a market maker may make an even higher offer, say 2.95, if he or she is a reluctant seller. If this offer is not taken by the broker, a market maker will typically next look to see what orders have been publicly declared to the pit by current brokers in other strikes. Suppose, for example, that an offer exists of some quantity of the 105 calls at .80, that is, five ticks over current fair-value price of 0.75. This offer may be a broker order posted on the board, or a verbal pit offer from another trader or broker that has not been posted. A market maker will always want to know the size of the offer, for this information is useful in knowing how much to trade against it in a spread. Unfortunately, brokers will not always divulge the size of an order, and estimates must sometimes be made.

If the offer of the 105 calls at 0.80 appears firm for 10 lots or more, the market maker can look to make a spread trade in March calls by separately lifting or buying the 105 call offer and hitting or selling the broker bid of 2.65 on the 100 calls if there appears to be enough profit in the spread trade.

To calculate the potential profitability of the spread trade, a market maker will determine the fair value of the 100–105 March call spread from the fair-value sheets, (Table 8.1), or $2.40 - 0.75 = 1.65$, when futures prices are trading at 100 and market implied volatility is 15. Since futures prices are hypothetically trading at 100, the only uncertainty is whether market implieds are likely to remain at 15.

Usually a market maker will have some idea whether the high broker bid on the 100 call represents a permanent shift in market implied volatility levels or is just a temporary high bid that will likely be soon hit. Let us assume the market maker believes the market level of implieds is likely to remain at 15 once the 100 call bid has been removed. Therefore, the 100–105 March call spread has a reasonable fair value at 1.65.

A typical reaction to the above situation, once these determinations have been made, is for a market maker to raise his or her bid on the 105 call from 0.70 (five under fair value) to 0.75 (fair value)

156 MARKET-MAKING TACTICS

to see if this bid will be hit by the trader or broker with the 105
calls to sell. If he or she can buy the 105 calls at 0.75 (fair value),
then he or she can immediately sell an equal quantity of the 100
calls at 2.65, thus selling the 100–105 call spread for a total of
1.90. This will represent selling the 100–105 call spread for 25
ticks over the fair value of the spread, that is, 1.90 − 1.65 = 0.25.
This spread will even be good if the market maker must pay the
offered 0.80 for the 105 call, since the spread will be sold for 1.85
versus the 1.65 fair value. In fact, if the implied spread levels
remained constant, a market maker may pay up to 0.95 for the
105 call and still make a small profit selling the 100 call at 2.65.

Depending on the quantities involved on each leg of the spread,
some delta adjustment must then be made. If each leg traded only
10 lots, then the market maker will need to buy about three futures
contracts to compensate for the larger amount of delta sold on the
100 calls than bought on the 105 calls [(10 × −.50) − (10 × .22) =
−2.80]. If the market maker had bought twenty-three 105 calls and
sold ten 100 calls (going long the ratio spread), no delta adjustment
with futures would be necessary.

If the market maker had sold the 100 calls outright at 2.65
and the implied volatility levels had remained at 15, he or she
would also have earned 25 ticks outright. The trader's delta neutrality would be maintained by going long one future for every
two at-the-money 100 calls sold short. But although the theoretical profit would be the same for selling the calls outright or selling
the spread, the former trade is only delta neutral, while the spread
trade is both delta and kappa/vega neutral. Thus, the spread trade
is vastly superior in terms of risk assumed.

Even if the settlement implied volatility has increased from
that of the market-maker fair-value sheets, this spread trade will
usually retain a net profit, although not so large. For example,
assume that the market implied volatility increases over the market maker fair-value sheets and that the 100 call settles at 2.65
when futures prices are 100. In this case, the market maker has
made no profit in selling the 100 calls at 2.65. However, by buying
the 105 calls at 0.75 (the old fair value) the market maker now
has a profit on this leg of the spread, for the increase in implied
volatilities will raise the fair value of the out-of-the-money calls
also (perhaps to 0.80 or 0.85). Even if the 100–105 call spread
is now trading at a higher fair value than 1.65 (say 1.80), the
market maker still will earn some profit by selling the spread at

1.90. Thus, by spread trading rather than selling calls outright, the market maker has protected himself or herself against kappa/vega risk, and has maintained the equilibrium of the basic carryover position.

Many traders think of spread trading in terms of the underlying implied levels, that is, buying 15 implieds on one leg and selling 15.5 on the other leg. In some option markets option prices may be given in terms of implied levels, (for example, 15 implied bid, offered at 15.3) instead of actual prices.

In general, once a spread trade is established or anticipated, a market maker has some power to lean into bids or lower offers in the different strikes, trade over or under fair value, and still expect to make a profit on the spread. Exactly how much over or under depends upon some assumptions concerning the implied volatility skew within the spread itself. The topic of skew will be taken up again in a following section.

Making a market with limited-risk spread tactics is somewhat like learning the steps in a dance, the left and right of hedged spread trading. It is seeing the different possibilities in price spreads that always exist in the pit and taking advantage of them. Good market making is seeing and trading spreads before they become obvious to other traders.

MAKING A TIME SPREAD MARKET

Consider the time spread prices for March and May calls in Table 8.1. Let us now assume that there exist a broker bid for the 95 March calls that is posted for 5.80, and a broker offer of the May 105 calls at 1.55 (see Table 8.3). If there is no current time basis spread between the March and May futures (that is, March and May trade at parity to each other), then the 95 March call bid is 15 ticks over fair value and the 105 May is offered at fair value.

Table 8.3   March/May call quote board

Calls	March	May
95	5.80 bid	
100		
105		1.55 asked

At these prices, it is not yet possible to do a limited-risk option spread between the 95 March and the 105 May calls (the 95–105 March/May call spread). Although there is a hypothetical profit of 15 ticks in buying the 105 May calls and selling the 95 March calls (buying the spread), the spread is a calendar spread and, therefore, needs to be hedged for time risk. Although the March/May futures basis spread is zero, there is no guarantee that this will remain so. Therefore, the trader of the March/May call spread will need to make an adjustment in delta in the absence of other option trading. The buyer of March/May will have to buy March and sell May futures to make delta more neutral with respect to time for buying May and selling March calls.

An option market maker usually gives up the edge in trading futures spreads, and futures spread markets are sometimes much wider than markets in single months. For these reasons, a market maker must lose some portion of his or her profit on the March/May call spread to trading the futures spread hedge. The original 0.15 gross profit on the call spread must be reduced to only 0.10 or 0.05 after futures trading adjustment has been made.

In Chapter 7 we considered the argument that delta adjustment on a time option spread adjusts for delta neutrality but not volatility neutrality. The buyer of March/May option spreads will be exposed to unlimited risk in the March/May volatility spread. If the short option month implied volatility levels increase dramatically over the long month implied levels, then the buyer of the March/May option spread will be exposed to potentially unlimited loss, which periodically happens to large buyers of option time spreads. Thus, in order to earn a 0.05–0.10 profit on a time spread option trade, a market maker would be exposed to catastrophic risk if he or she adjusted for time only with futures contracts.

The only secure option time spread cannot be completed at the prices in Table 8.3. A market maker would look to complete March/May spreads separately (by buying other March calls against the short 95 March calls or selling other May calls to buy the 105 May offer), or to trade the March/May spread in some other way.

Brokers sometimes bid or ask for option time spreads that offer astute market makers opportunities for profit. Let us assume as before that there exist a 5.80 bid for the 95 March call and a 1.55 offer for the 105 May call, with both futures remaining at 100. Now, suppose a broker bids 1.10 for the March/May 100 call spread, that is, offers to buy the May call 1.10 points over the sale of the March call. Can a market maker trade profitably at these prices?

To determine whether this is a good trade, a trader will consider that the fair value of the March/May 100 call spread is .95 May over March (3.35 − 2.40). By offering to pay up to 1.10 May over March, the broker is bidding 15 ticks over the fair value of the option time spread. As with the the March/May 95–105 call spread above, there is no advantage in doing the March/May 100 call spread alone because of the reduced profit after time spread and futures delta hedging costs have been subtracted and because of the unlimited risk exposure.

However, by trading the March/May 100 and 95–105 call spreads together at the above prices, a market maker can earn a good profit and assume no unlimited time risk. A good market maker will sell the May 100 calls (at 3.50) and buy the March 100 calls (at 2.40) for a time spread of 1.10, and simultaneously buy the 105 May calls and sell the 95 March calls that are posted. The completed trades will look like this:

Sell March 95 calls at 5.80 (15 ticks over fair value)
Buy March 100 calls at 2.40 (fair value)

Sell May 100 calls at 3.50 (15 ticks over fair value)
Buy May 105 calls at 1.55 (fair value)

The gross profit on these trades is 0.30, assuming a one-to-one ratio of purchases to sales. Since the spread trades are completed as noncalendar spreads, no futures time spread adjustment is required, although some futures adjustment may still be necessary in each month separately. In this example, a trader would most likely have to buy both March and May futures in some small amounts to remain delta neutral, unless he or she traded some ratio spreads. Thus, the gross profit of .30 will be little diminished. In executing these trades a market maker has completed two separate noncalendar spreads that need minimal time spread delta or kappa/vega adjustments.

These kinds of spread opportunities are what a market maker must look out for. A novice option trader may wish to practice calculating option spreads in his or her head until it becomes second nature. Also, traders will find it advantageous to remember broker spread orders that did not get filled immediately; they usually are not posted although they may remain current. With a sudden market move, these broker spreads may become tradable for a spread scalper.

Unfortunately, much of the time it is not possible to do simultaneous offsetting time spread trades, or even vertical spreads, without legging them. Legging spreads has a limited risk in normal volatility periods only if the long side is put on first, then the short side.

There are traders who do attempt to leg spreads by going short first. To the greater risk goes the greater profit—but also the greater (potential) loss. Trading in this way will sooner or later produce financial catastrophe. Legging spreads as well as putting on any new position is best done by going long, then short in a leapfrog sort of way.

How long to go on the first leg? This is a subjective judgment; 20 lots is large to some, small to others. An option trader will want to avoid too large a time decay on the first leg of a time spread, but here again what is large to one is not to another. Some traders will always do a size of 100 or more, even in a narrowly liquid option pit.

Some tactical issues facing spread traders have been discussed in the last two sections. Good option market making is essentially good vertical and time spread trading.

POSITION DELTA ADJUSTMENTS

If the delta-neutral limited-risk strategy has proved successful, a trader is confronted with maintaining the delta-neutrality and limited risk of nonsynthetic positions. To stay delta-neutral, the trader usually must make small continual adjustments in the option carryover position and any new trades. A change in futures prices almost invariably changes an option's delta, and this will throw the position off delta neutrality, requiring some adjustment to be made eventually. If the trader is long two at-the-money 100 calls and short one future, the trader will be delta-neutral. When futures move to 110, however, the trader will now be net long delta, for example.

But position delta can change even if futures prices do not. There is some tendency for the net delta of an option position to shift over time, gradually in the back months and more abruptly in the front months. A change in the implied volatilities of an option will also usually change an option's delta. There are several reasons for this *delta drift*.

First, the passage of time means that the standard deviation will shrink, all else being equal. A smaller standard deviation will also shrink the delta value for an out-of-the-money option and increase the delta for an in-the-money option (while the at-the-money option will always remain at .50).

For example, a long 100–110 vertical call spread that has a net delta of about .30 in the back months when futures are at 100 will increase to about .40–.45 delta in the front months if volatility remains constant and futures remain at 100. The long 100 call will retain +.50 delta but the negative delta of the 110 call will shrink over time; thus the total delta of the call spread will assymptotically approach +.50. For small option positions, this daily delta drift is negligible, but for large positions delta drift may mean that a market maker's carryover position is going long or short several futures contracts with the passage of every day.

Second, the delta of an option position will also be affected by changes in the implied volatility levels. Intuitively, one expects that the out-of-the-money or the in-the-money option time premium will be affected by how likely it is that the option will end in-the-money. A higher implied or real volatility level will increase the likelihood of expiring in-the-money and, all else being equal, will affect the delta of the option. An increase in implied volatility will increase the delta of an out-of-the-money option and decrease the delta of an in-the-money option.

In summary, the passage of time and changes in the implied volatility levels will affect the total position delta. This position delta change is termed *delta drift*. In general, the total net delta of a vertical spread will more nearly resemble the delta of the near- or at-the-money strike option closer to expiration and the lower the implied volatility level. The occurrence of delta drift requires some adjustment trading on a periodic or even a daily basis in order to maintain delta-neutrality.

To keep track of required position delta adjustments, an option trader must know what his or her position delta is at all times, and what it would be under different changing market conditions. To track delta, one usually uses position analysis software, since market-maker carryover positions may grow so large that they are not easily analyzed by manual calculation. With software, however, it is easy to track position delta under different time and volatility assumptions and identify what adjustments must be made. Because of time spread risk, it is important to analyze position delta on a single calendar month separately—that is, without time spreads included.

A position delta analysis for a hypothetical option position under different market price, volatility and time assumptions is shown in Table 8.4. With futures at 100 and implied volatility at 15 on the current day, the net position delta is neutral (as indicated by *). However, position delta will change as futures prices move up (position delta long 10 at 104) or down (−10 at 96). Position delta will also often change for large positions if there is a shift in the level of market implied volatilities (a +1.00 shift in delta for a +1.00-unit shift in implied volatility level). Finally, in the example the passage of one day will lower the net position delta by one, all else being equal. A delta drift, or changes in any one of these factors (futures, implieds, or time), will often necessitate some trade adjustment if delta neutrality is to be maintained on the carryover position.

Of course, during the day a market maker will be doing additional trades that affect position delta. Market makers routinely keep a cumulative net delta tally of trades during the day. When it is added to the net delta of the carryover position, a trader should know to a close approximation his or her total net position delta without continually entering all trades into the computer right when they occur. A midday exact update would be prudent in busy trading, though.

Table 8.4 Position delta

| | Implied Volatility Levels | | | |
| | Current Day | | Next Day | |
Futures Prices	15	16	15	16
104	10	11	9	10
102	5	6	4	5
100	0*	1	−1	0
98	−5	−4	−6	−5
96	−10	−9	−11	−10

gamma = +2.5.

*Net position delta is neutral.

Combining the information from the carryover position delta based on futures prices and implied levels with the net delta of the daily trades, a market maker will strive for delta neutrality. At this point the tactics of adjustment diverge, depending upon whether the carryover position is net long or short gamma/kappa/vega/theta. These will be discussed over the next several sections.

GAMMA TRADING

Any non-synthetic option position will have either a negative or a positive gamma risk exposure. In Chapter 4 we found that negative gamma in single-month positions is always associated with negative kappa/vega and positive theta. Positive gamma is always associated with positive kappa/vega and negative theta. Since gamma represents the change in net delta for a fixed change in asset price, gamma trading is concerned with adjusting net delta after an asset price change has occurred. A positive or negative gamma stance will require different adjustment tactics, discussed below.

The only delta-neutral limited-risk strategy that is partially negative gamma is the long butterfly. Keeping a butterfly strictly at delta neutrality at all times is very difficult since using futures to adjust large butterflies will alter the structure of the butterfly itself. Unless balanced by one-to-one spread trades, a butterfly will quickly become either a catastrophic risk position if too many options are sold or a long ratio spread or wrangle if too many are bought. As a practical matter, therefore, a trader who makes markets on a strict butterfly carryover is rare. Nevertheless, these guidelines for delta adjustment of the long butterfly will serve generally for near-butterflies or other partially negative gamma/kappa/vega, positive theta positions.

The adjustment tactic for any negative gamma strategy if futures prices are rising and a negative delta is accumulating is to buy calls, sell puts, or buy futures. Each of these trade actions will add positive delta to the carryover position. If the market is falling and a positive delta is accumulating, the trader will look to buy puts, sell calls, or sell futures, thereby adding negative delta to the carryover position. Negative gamma tactics trade with the trend to adjust delta.

Using futures contracts to maintain delta neutrality is probably the least desirable. Aside from (usually) losing the edge in the futures pit, outright futures positions expose the trader to the possibility of frequent whipsaw losses during the day and can be very frustrating to trade. Short gamma traders are usually the ones to buy the high and sell the low of the day's futures prices. Yet, not adjusting will at times incur even greater losses, and futures are often the first means of delta adjustment in the market.

A better way to adjust delta is to use options rather than futures, and get the edge doing so. However, a trader will not always be presented with the opportunity to buy puts directly in a falling market with the edge, or to buy calls in rising markets in positive theta ranges.

Presumably, in falling markets the demand for puts means that a market maker will be pressed to sell puts rather than be afforded the opportunity to buy them. Likewise in rising markets, market makers may be asked to sell calls rather than be allowed the opportunity to buy them. Of course, if it is not possible to buy puts in a falling market or buy calls in a rising market with the edge, it will also not be possible to sell futures synthetically (buy the put, sell the call) in falling markets or buy futures synthetically (buy the call, sell the put) in a rising market.

The most favorable delta adjustment in trending markets occurs when puts or calls are mispriced with respect to each other, and it is possible to buy (or sell) the cheaper (or more expensive) and turn it into an opposite put or call synthetically. In falling markets puts may be overpriced and calls underpriced at fair values to each other, and in rising markets calls may trade over the fair value of puts.

Thus, in a falling market it is often possible to buy calls cheaply, as others rush to sell, and, by selling futures contracts simultaneously, to buy a long put synthetically. Likewise, by buying undervalued puts on the upside and as well as a futures contract, the trader has bought a long call synthetically that is often cheaper than the actual call. In this way a market maker can maintain delta neutrality and at the same time earn a reasonable profit with the edge.

How much delta adjustment should a trader in a negative gamma position make over small future price changes? There is probably no way to answer this question with complete certainty. The size of gamma is the measure of the risk the trader takes by not adjusting delta. The appropriate size of gamma risk cannot be predetermined for every position, but depends in part on the size of the trader's capital and on the trader's ability to sustain an occasional series of small and sometimes large losses. An unlimited-risk negative gamma trader, however, unlike a positive gamma trader, will eventually be forced to adjust position delta to avoid extremely large or catastrophic losses.

One thing a short gamma trader should not do as a delta adjustment is to sell only options, whether puts or calls. Selling options only will increase the negative gamma and expose the trader to increasing catastrophic risk.

As a matter of course, positive gamma/kappa/vega, negative theta strategies (also known as *long premium strategies*) will face situations in which, as futures prices rise, the position becomes increasingly long delta; and, as prices fall, increasingly short delta. To remain delta neutral on the upside, a trader will sell futures, buy puts, or sell calls, which will add negative position delta. Likewise, on the downside the trader will buy futures, sell puts, or buy calls to add positive delta. Since the long gamma trader will be selling calls and buying puts in a rising market and selling puts and buying calls in a falling market, the astute market maker can also earn an extra profit if the same strike put/call market is trading at a premium/discount relationship. In any case, these adjustments may be used to re-establish delta neutrality.

Sometimes the long gamma trader can let the delta *run* in one direction or the other, following the trend of the market. If a market maker does not adjust to delta neutrality and the market continues to run further in one direction, the profits to the long gamma trader may become considerable. For this reason a trader who is long gamma may not always wish to adjust to delta neutrality as a tactic, unlike the negative gamma trader. This flexibility in delta adjustment, open to the long gamma trader, is referred to as *gamma trading*.

For example, assume that a long gamma trader is initially delta neutral, but during the day the futures prices stage a big rally. This rally increases the net position delta from neutrality to +5 delta points and the trader, in effect, is long the equivalent of five futures contracts. The long gamma trader has a paper profit from the rally in futures prices.

The question of whether to lock in this profit or to let it run must be faced by any long gamma trader. On the one hand, by letting delta continue to run in the direction of futures prices without adjustment, a trader may accumulate very large profits if futures prices move in one direction or another in a big move. On the other hand, if the trader does not lock in the profit (by selling five futures contracts), and the rally fails and futures prices move back to where they began, then the trader will show no profit from this temporary gyration in the market. If the trader had sold the five futures to lock in the profit, the decline in futures prices would not affect this profit since when futures prices had finished retracing themselves, the short futures would be covered and the long gamma position restored to its original condition.

In choppy markets, gamma trading comes into its own. By adjusting delta frequently during the course of a wildly gyrating market, a long gamma trader may make very large profits, even if futures prices settle unchanged for the day. Getting whipsawed is no problem for the long gamma trader, who will often be selling at the top and buying at the bottom.

There is no exact answer to the question of when to readjust to delta neutrality in the event of a futures price move. Small positive gamma positions may require little or no delta adjustment for many trading days as prices remain in narrow ranges. In the event of a large price move, however, adjustment becomes more pressing.

What constitutes a large enough price move to adjust delta? There can be no definitive or absolute answer. It depends as much upon a trader's style as anything else. At some point in an extreme daily price move, it is probably wise for long kappa/vega traders to lock in some profit by delta neutralization and secure the profits already made. In wildly active markets that are going up and down, gamma trading these whipsaws can be very profitable.

Of course, limit move days must be considered the best outcome for long gamma strategies, since the market moves furthest and little delta adjustment may be possible or needed as profits accumulate. Perhaps once every five to ten years, most commodities will experience a truly phenomenal move, with limit days in one direction strung together in a run. Although only exposed to limited risk, a long gamma trader at these times may earn spectacular returns, as discussed in the section of Chapter 7 dealing with trading high volatility.

ADJUSTMENT OF THETA (Θ)/KAPPA (K)/VEGA

In addition to delta and gamma adjustment, large option positions usually require ongoing theta and kappa/vega risk adjustment. As noted in Chapter 3, these risks are related. Single-month option positions that are positive kappa/vega are always negative theta, and negative kappa/vega positions are always positive theta. Also, the absolute sizes of kappa/vega and theta risk are linked over time. Kappa/vega risk is greatest furthest from expiration and least at expiration, whereas theta risk is always highest at expiration and least furthest from expiration. There is a time drift to kappa/vega and theta risks that may often require adjustment for this reason even if nothing else has changed.

Basic strategy calls for a limited-risk profile with respect to kappa/vega. Thus, aside from the butterfly position, market makers will tend to be positive kappa/vega and negative theta, that is, long volatility during normal volatility periods. The prudence of long volatility will be more valuable when expiration is furthest away and when kappa/vega risk is at its highest. Generally, back- and middle-month LRO-DN positions must pay more attention to kappa/vega, and near-front-month positions to theta. But any strategy is cautious about becoming too long kappa/vega, especially at high levels. A smart strategy seeks to avoid catastrophic risk at all times, to profit by real or implied volatility explosions, and to limit time decay loss.

But how much long kappa/vega risk is appropriate in back-month positions? The answer depends upon trader risk assumptions and will vary. A conservative rule of thumb is not to be long more kappa/vega than a trader could reduce to neutrality in one or two days. The number of options required to establish neutrality will generally increase over time as kappa/vega risk falls towards expiration. For example, a sale of 10 at-the-money options may move the kappa/vega risk of the entire position by $1,000 at 100 days to expiration, but the same sale will change the kappa/vega risk by only $500 at 50 days to expiration.

A very high positive kappa/vega risk for a long wrangle would resemble a long straddle, which has been seen to have some disadvantages. How large a kappa/vega risk in dollar or percentage terms will depend to some extent upon the size of the trader's capital, the average volume in the pit, and a trader's taste for at least some risk.

As back-month positions become front-month positions, the negative theta on long ratio spreads and long wrangles will become increasingly costly. At that time the trader should think of bringing the wrangle closer to a butterfly/condor. Exactly how much theta risk to carry in the front-month positions also depends upon trader assumptions about risk and market.

Maintaining a positive or neutral theta is perhaps one of the more difficult challenges an option trader faces near expiration because at that time the public is often a net seller of at-the-money options in many option markets. This same situation confronts stock option market makers, who also must take the long side of the public's preference for covered call writing.

To maintain a positive or neutral theta in the center strikes, an option trader must buy as many contracts as he or she is selling. Option traders may want (1) to lower their bids slightly below fair value to avoid attempting to support sagging prices induced by net public selling close to expiration and (2) to avoid too much net buying. For traders positive kappa/vega closer to expiration, some net selling of options may be necessary on an ongoing basis to curtail the increasing loss due to time decay.

As with position delta analysis, position kappa/vega/theta analysis commonly relies on computer software. On such software a typical single-month position analysis might look like Table 8.5. This hypothetical position would be positive kappa/vega and negative theta in the dollar amounts shown for a range of futures prices. For example, when futures are at 100, this position will profit $1,000 by a one-point increase in market implied levels but lose $300 per day on time decay. This position would present a

Table 8.5   Position kappa/vega and theta: Example I

Futures Price ($)	Kappa	Theta
104	+2000	−500
102	+1000	−300
100	+1000	−300
98	+1000	−300
96	+2400	−700

bidirectional limited kappa/vega risk profile, which is consistent with basic prudent strategy.

A problem that may frequently develop for a market maker careless about strategy is a directional lopsided kappa/vega risk. That is, position kappa/vega risk changes sign with futures price change. Such a position might look like Table 8.6. This hypothetical position has a bimodal kappa/vega/theta risk profile; the downside has limited kappa/vega risk, but the upside has unlimited risk. This position is characteristic of vertical spreads, fences, or cartwheel strategies, which have bimodal kappa/vega risk.

A bimodal kappa/vega risk position often may develop if a trader is doing too many *fences* with brokers, that is, selling calls and buying puts that are not of the same strike. Doing fences without separate adjustment of the put and call spread will lead a trader into a bimodal kappa/vega risk position eventually. When a bi-modal position becomes apparent, a trader will tactically try to buy options on the short kappa/vega wing until the problem is corrected. These purchases must be made as soon as possible, for the wing that is short kappa/vega also exposes the trader to catastrophic risk.

One way to obtain a rough idea of how much bimodal kappa/vega risk a position is carrying is to notice the net futures in the carryover position that are not part of synthetics. A large net-futures carryover that is not synthetically based is probably a lopsided kappa/vega risk position.

Of course, a trader will sometimes, through an inadvertent sale of options, become short kappa/vega on both wings. In a sense, a trader tips his or her own canoe and inverts the risk profile. This

Table 8.6 Position kappa/vega and theta: Example II

Futures Price ($)	Kappa	Theta
104	−500	+500
102	−300	+200
100	0	0
98	+300	−200
96	+700	−500

---

situation is even more serious than a bimodal kappa/vega risk position, since now the position is catastrophically risk exposed both on the upside and on the downside in futures prices. A short kappa/vega position can only be corrected by the purchase of puts or calls, straddles or strangles, which traders should do quickly to remain risk limited.

WATCHING THE IMPLIEDS

Among option traders there is great interest in knowing what direction implied volatility levels are headed. A market maker will always know where the current implied levels are, especially for the at-the-money straddle. But knowing where the implieds are does not identify where they are going. Knowing the direction of implied volatilities for an option trader is like knowing the direction of price for a futures trader. There are several ways of following implied volatility trends.

Sometimes charts and moving averages of implied levels are used to give some idea of the future, or at least current, direction of implied volatility. Something simple will usually be sufficient to alert the market maker to the primary trend. Many exchanges regularly publish time charts on historical volatility as shown in previous chapters, and, of course, market makers will have the daily results of implied levels, which can be charted easily.

Option traders will also want to know any past seasonal variations in implied levels that are due to change of crop season or other factors. In many seasonal crop futures, real and implied volatility levels may be higher when carryover stocks are lowest, at the transition from old crop to new crop. Once the new harvest is in, stocks are replenished and volatility may seasonally go down, which is the case in soybean implied volatilities noted by Christopher Bobin (1990). (See Figure 8.1.)

Whatever method of following implied volatility trends he or she uses, an option market maker is most likely first to know of an implied volatility change through daily trading on the floor. As noted in Chapter 7, following broker net order flows will give the trader some idea of the supply/demand for options and, therefore, the likely current trend and direction of implied levels.

If it becomes increasingly difficult for a trader to do both legs of an option spread, and if repeated failure to leg spreads is giving the total carryover position a lopsided kappa/vega (short or long) while

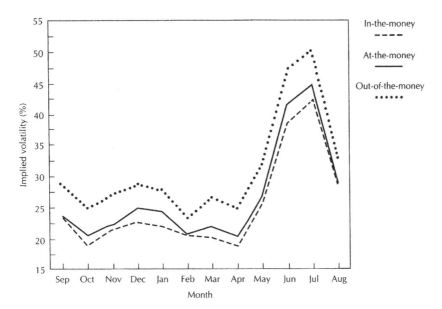

Figure 8.1 Average monthly soybean implied volatility, 1986–1988. (*Source:* Christopher A. Bobin, 1990, *Agricultural Options: Trading, Risk, and Management,* New York: John Wiley and Sons, Inc.)

awaiting the completion of the spread, then the side of the spread that the trader is having trouble completing indicates the next direction of implied levels. Some traders develop a keen pit sense of implied volatility change in this way through spread trading.

SKEW RISK REVISITED

An option trader will always want to know where the at-the-money straddle is trading, both in dollars and as an implied volatility. The at-the-money straddle will set the center of the skew of market implied volatility. Skew is the difference between the at-the-money implied levels and the implied levels in the remaining strikes. There are two skews: a put skew and a call skew. Out-of-the-money options often trade at higher implied volatilities than at-the-money options; that is, there is a positive skew for both puts and calls. Since these skews need not remain constant, they represent skew risk to any vertical spread trade.

The degree of skew often appears to be directly related to different option expiration cycles. That is, options that are the furthest to expiration (more than six months) are likely to reflect fair values close to the BSM model over the lowest and highest strikes traded and, therefore, present a flat skew. Options in the middle range to expiration (from three to six months) have a saucer-shaped positive skew, and the near-term options (less than three months) begin to resemble a steep bowl-shaped positive skew over the lowest and highest strikes on the board (Figure 8.2).

Negative skew is generally rare during any expiration cycle for most options markets. The most important exception is stock and stock index options, where there is often a persistent negative call skew.

Market makers usually seek to replicate these implied skews (positive or negative), as identified from raw data, in printing fair-value sheets or in making markets practically. It can be shown, however, that the difference in time skews is, at least in part, more apparent than real. What the raw implied time skews do not take into account is the relative distance between strikes. The distance between a 100 and a 110 strike with a year to expiration is not the same as when there is only a month to expiration. The reason is that futures prices may easily move the distance between two wide strikes with lots of time, but be very unlikely to do so with little time remaining.

To compensate for time differences in implied skew, one can measure skew in a standardized vertical and horizontal scale.

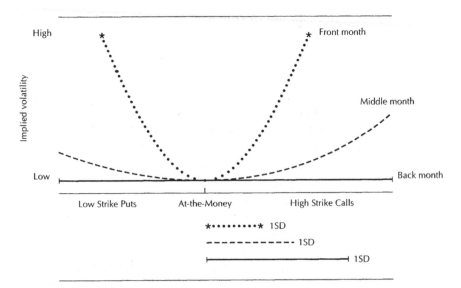

Figure 8.2 Implied volatility skew, unstandardized.

Two modifications may be made. First, the raw implied levels may be recalculated by dividing the wing strike implied by the at-the-money implied levels. These calculations will give a series of skew BSM implied relative levels that may be used in place of the absolute levels. For example, if the implied of a 105 wing strike is 15.75 and the 100 center strike is 15, then the implied relative is 15.75/15 = 1.05. That is, the 105 strike carries a 1.05 BSM implied relative to the 100 strike.

Second, a more important modification is to standardize the horizontal scale of strikes. This may easily be accomplished by measuring strike distance between wings and the center in terms of standard deviations (SDs) of futures prices. For instance, with a 15 implied volatility, futures prices at 100, and 41 days to expiration, the SD will be just over five futures points. Thus, the 105 strike in this example will be just about one SD from the 100 strike. With only 10 days to expiration, however, with all other assumptions the same, the 105 strike will be about two SDs from the 100 strike.

When implied skews are measured in terms of standard deviations (SDs) along the vertical scale, much of the apparent differences between time skews disappears. To show this, consider a time option series in which the back months have an SD of 10, the middle months an SD of 5, and the front month an SD of 2.50. If the implied relatives are 1.05 at one SD and 1.15 at two SDs, then the empirical time differences of implied skew in Figure 8.2 will disappear. This fact may quickly be verified by noting that when the SD = 10, the 110 strike has an implied volatility of 15.75 (a 1.05 implied relative); when the SD = 5, the 105 strike also has an implied of 15.75, and so on. Despite the diversity of different time implied skews, all skews when standardized are taken from only one adjusted skew model. Variations in empirical cycle skews will greatly diminish after one has adjusted for time and standard deviation, as illustrated in Figure 8.3.

Even though standardization reduces empirical skew risk, it is not eliminated entirely. The existence of a standardized implied volatility skew presents a theoretical problem to the BSM fair-value model. The market seems consistently to overprice out-of-the-money options relative to at-the-money options. Essentially, market participants evaluate options from a probability standpoint unlike that used by the BSM model; traders seem to assign greater risk to more extreme futures price moves than the normal curve

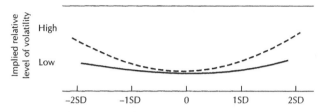

Figure 8.3   Standardized implied volatility skew.

suggests. In the jargon of statistical theory, the empirical distribution has thicker tails than normal and is platykurtic.

There has been much interest in developing alternative statistical models of futures price change that do not depend on the normal curve. These can be used to produce other fair-value option models than the BSM model, with binomial or more complex interest rate structures as discussed in Chapter 2. In the optimum outcome some alternative fair-value models could eliminate some of the existing implied skew from the BSM model and possibly eliminate the data-normal error curve itself.

In a perfect option model, there would be no standardized implied skew at all, but it is unlikely that such perfection will be achieved, even in the best-constructed alternative models. Recognition of this improbability arises because the time-adjusted empirical BSM skew itself is not constant over time but *wobbles,* with implied relative volatilities rising or falling with no corresponding change in futures standard deviation. Despite standardization, there is instability in the skew implied relatives. Sometimes the wings trade at a greater standardized implied relative to the center than at other times (all else being equal). Thus, at 1 SD the implied relative may be 1.05 on one day but at 1.07 the next, without the at-the-money implied levels having changed.

Wobble in skew poses an investment risk to any vertical spread trader. Large market-maker carryover positions are particularly subject to wobble risk insofar as they are composed of many spread positions. Since a spread is always the trade of two different strike options, skew will always be an important factor in evaluating the fair-value of the spread. Wobble in skew translates into wobble in spread fair-values, which may cause serious financial consequences for large spread traders.

Consider the fair-value of a 100–105 call spread, with 60 days to expiration, an interest rate of 7 percent, a futures price of 100, and an implied volatility for the 100 call at constant 15 with the 100 call valued at 2.40. At an implied volatility of 15 (flat skew) the 105 call has a fair-value of 0.74; at an implied volatility of 16 (low positive skew) the 105 call has a fair-value of 0.86, and at an implied volatility of 17 (high positive skew) the 105 call is worth 0.98.

The fair-values of the 100–105 (1×1 and 1×2) call spreads under these different skews are found in Table 8.7. If a trader were to buy the 100–105 (1×1) call spread (buy the 100, sell the 105 calls) when skew was flat at 1.66, then a loss could accrue if the skew went from flat to low or high positive skew ($1.54 − $1.66 = −0.12 and $1.42 − $1.66 = −0.24). If the trader were to short the ratio spread by buying the the 100 call and selling the 105 call twice (1×2), the results financially would be even worse as skew moves from flat to low to high positive (0.68 − 0.92 = −0.24 and 0.44 − 0.92 = −0.48).

From the standpoint of skew risk, it is not a good idea to be a buyer of bullish call or bearish put spreads when skew is flat, or to attempt to short the ratio spread. Rather, selling option (1×1) spreads and going long the ratio spreads during flat skew periods is a better strategy. During periods of high positive skew relatives, it is better to buy option spreads and cover any short spreads or long ratio spreads. A long wrangle will experience a profit going from a flat to a high skew but a loss going from high to flat skew.

For large traders (with many hundreds or thousands of contracts and spreads), a skew wobble in the implied relatives can translate into thousands of dollars of fluctuations in an option account balance on a daily basis. Spread positions will experience

Table 8.7   100–105 Call spread values by skew

	Spread (dollar value)	
Skew	(1×1)	(1×2)
Flat	1.66	.92
Low positive	1.54	.68
High positive	1.42	.44

(See Table 5.3 for underlying option prices.)

wobble fluctuations in daily profit and loss accounts. Failure to take into account wobble can mean a market maker taking on spread trades that will later prove overpriced even when there is no change in the at-the-money implied volatility or futures prices!

The best way for a market maker to ensure that this does not happen is to be aware of the ranges for skew relatives on the particular option contract in which he or she is making a market and attempt to spread trade accordingly. A trader would try not to pay more for wing options than flat or low skew prices, and would attempt to sell or liquidate positions during high skew prices, all else being equal.

A further difficulty in skew risk is that the center strikes of the skew will change in a large asset or futures price move, thus moving or shifting the entire skew itself, as in Figure 8.4.

A shift in skew may significantly affect the value of vertical spreads and is a risk to the complex spread trader. For example, if a trader executed a short 100 strike and a long 110 strike call spread when skew is centered at 100 strike then a futures/asset price move to 110 will shift the entire skew so that the short call is now at the high point on skew and the 110 call will be at the center strike. In effect, even though skew remained positive after the shift, the call spread would have suffered the same financial effects as if skew had gone from positive to negative!

The effects of skew wobble occurring simultaneously with skew shift may be additive and present some significant risk to any complex option vertical spread trader. Moreover, there is no perfect way to hedge complex vertical spreads against skew wobble and shift risk, short of synthetic trading. Nevertheless, although it is

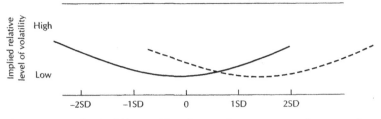

Figure 8.4 Skew shift resulting from a large asset or futures price move upward.

an important risk, skew risk is not unlimited, fortunately. In the end, market judgment and cautious experience may be the best guides.

TRACKING TRADING RESULTS

A market maker will usually be able to tell whether he or she is trading successfully by whether he or she is making a profit over the long run. Clearinghouses will provide a trader with a daily net account balance that gives the final tally. It is useful, however, for a market maker to keep his or her own financial accounts, independent of clearinghouse records. There are several reasons for doing this.

First, keeping independent accounts can be used to verify clearinghouse records. Although intentional mistakes are rare, clearinghouse records often show clerical errors, sometimes of a large magnitude. Without an independent account record, a trader is sometimes helpless to correct clearinghouse statements. If the clearinghouse statement remains uncorrected, which sometimes happens, a trader may incur a large windfall loss.

Second, without an independent account to highlight clearinghouse account inaccuracies, a trader will not know his or her exact position and cannot adjust properly or know the risks he or she is under. There will always be traders on any exchange who do not know their exact position because of clearinghouse confusion, and who then take a large hit, sometimes even being wiped out.

Third, keeping an independent account gives the trader the ability to track and analyze trading results. Although one might assume that overall profitability is an indication of market-making success, this need hardly be the case. Market-maker profitability must be distinguished from overall profitability if a market maker wishes to assess accurately his or her own trading success (or loss).

For accounting purposes, total profit/loss (P/L) may be divided into that P/L resulting from the carryover position, and that P/L from daily trades. To show the daily P/L for the carryover position, mark the value of the position to settlement prices at end of Day 1 and Day 2 without adding new trades, and take the difference. This will represent the P/L due to the carryover position over one day. To show the daily P/L due to new trading, subtract the prices of the option at trade from the settlement prices for that day. The daily P/L due to the carryover position when added to the daily trade P/L will equal the total P/L of the position.

The net daily carryover P/L corresponds to the P/L of the limited-risk strategy itself, while the daily trade P/L will show the results due to market making. A market-maker will be trading successfully if the market-making profits are a large or the largest share of total profits over the long run.

Consider the P/L separately for the daily carryover account and the daily trading account, as in Table 8.8. The total profit for the combined carryover and day trades in Table 8.8 is +1, but this is entirely contributed by the day trade results. To do the next

Table 8.8   Example of total profit/loss statement for a hypothetical market maker

Daily Carryover Account				
Carryover and Prices	Settlement Day 1	Settlement Day 2	End Day 2 Profit/Loss	
100 short 100 calls	2.00	2.10	−10.	
100 long 100 puts	1.00	.90	−10.	
Long 100 futures	.80	1.00	+20.	
Subtotal profit			+20.	−20.
Total carryover profit			zero	

Daily Trading Account			
Day Trades and Prices	Day 2 Trade Price	Settlement Day 2	End Day 2 Profit/Loss
Sell 10, 100 calls	2.20	2.10	+1
Buy 10 futures	100	100	zero
Subtotal profit			+1
Day trading profit			+1

Net Profits by Activity	
Carryover position	zero
Day trades	+1
Total net profit	+1

day, the net day trades by strike and option are added to or subtracted from the carryover position, and a new carryover position is established for the next day carryover position accounting, plus whatever next day trading occurs.

A trader may wish to refine the analysis of P/L for the carryover position further by doing each cycle separately. With an ongoing daily record of this accounting, a more detailed P/L record is visible. For example, consider the daily P/L accounts in Table 8.9. In this Table, the net result of the May, July, and December positions is −$100 ($0 − 150 + 50), largely stemming from the poor July cycle results. This result is not necessarily too serious since many monthly position P/Ls will show short-term deviations that balance out over time. A trader would, of course, want to examine the larger July loss in this example to see whether it represents a poorly hedged position or just reflects daily irregularities in settlements, which quickly adjust themselves.

In Table 8.9, the net result of the carryover positions was −$100, but profits from daily scalping were $300, giving a total net profit of $200. With daily market making contributing a large share of gross and net profits, one may infer that this trader is market making successfully but might be able to improve results by adjusting the carryover position.

The accounting assumption that day trade net results are attributable to market making over the long run is probably valid. Although the daily net trading profits may also be attributable to gamma adjustment tactics, over the long run these daily gamma adjustments should net to zero against daily carryover position changes, leaving the remainder of the daily P/L as net market-making profits. Thus, it remains true that a positive net P/L total over the long run on the daily trading account is an approximate

Table 8.9 Daily P/L by component

Day	Carryovers ($)			Day Trading Net ($)	Net Total ($)
	May	July	December		
1	−100	−200	+300	+ 50	+ 50
2	+100	+100	−200	+250	+250
3	0	− 50	− 50	0	−100
Total	0	−150	+ 50	+300	+200

indication of market-making profitability if a trader has remained delta neutral in the carryover position.

If over a longer period a trader's total profits are largely contributed by day trade results, then a market maker is trading well. If this is not the case, or the trader is losing money on net balance, then looking at the accounting results separately by day trade and carryover position will help diagnose the problem by indicating where loss is occurring.

COMMON MISTAKES

Mistakes are inevitable. Since market makers and scalpers work for a small arbitrage profit, however, even small mistakes can mean the difference between profit and loss. Although mistakes are inevitable, they should be minimized as much as possible.

What are the most frequent mistakes option traders make? There are at least four areas in which traders probably err repeatedly. These are:

1. Failure to hedge delta

2. Incorrect delta hedging

3. Overtrading

4. Poor kappa/vega risk adjustment

Failure to Hedge Delta (Δ)

Not maintaining delta neutrality is probably the single most frequent mistake an option scalper will make. The best type of option scalping is spread trading, but when this is not immediately available an option trader must hedge delta to remain delta neutral. Many traders, however, do not immediately execute delta adjustments in the futures market after doing a nonspread option trade. This is a mistake. *Taking a shot* is, in fact, speculation, and market makers who do not hedge their delta risk immediately are speculating.

The lure to speculate by not futures hedging one's option trades immediately is strong. By attempting to get the edge on the futures side, a market maker can often double the profit of the trade. This will happen just often enough to yield positive reinforcement for the trader to continue to avoid immediately hedging futures.

In the instances in which the trader does not get the edge, and does not get his or her futures hedge off, the market may (and probably will) move against the trader on the unhedged option side, causing losses instead of profits. If an option trader were willing to accept a loss immediately, the losses and profits would probably balance out to neutral in the long run, perhaps giving the trader the false impression that speculation is, at worst, neutral.

But what often happens is that an option trader is not willing to take a small loss to hedge when it will mean a small loss on the original trade. Eventually these small losses turn into large losses. In speculating by not hedging immediately or at all, many option traders cut their profits short, but let their losses run. For these traders, market-making profits are eaten up very quickly in speculative losses.

The best course is to avoid speculation, and to hedge delta whenever any option trade is completed that is not an option spread trade. If a trader waits to hedge delta in the best way, the outcome may be large losses. *Hedge when you should, not when it is best.*

Incorrect Delta (Δ) Hedging

Poor delta hedging entails trading options at prices that are unrealistic compared with the current futures price at which delta hedges may be traded. In other words, hedges cannot be done at posted futures prices because the board prices for some reason are lagging behind actual pit trading. If a market maker is limited to using futures prices as posted on the board to price options, he or she will be at a disadvantage and risk trading options at unrealistic futures prices. There are several ways to avoid this trap.

One way is to stand physically close enough to the futures pit to hear futures trading. If an option trader is able to do this, then he or she can hear, and even do, futures trades while trading options. But in large futures and options rings, where there is greater physical distance between the futures and options pits, it will not always be possible for an option trader to be near the futures ring. In this situation, a clerk may be necessary to signal by hand futures prices to the trader and to relay futures orders to the futures pit. This must be considered an added cost of business.

Another aspect of unrealistic futures pricing should be mentioned. It is best not to be last in a string of large option trades in the pit, in order to avoid being in an infavorable futures hedging position. Brokers will sometimes come into the ring and immediately do a large quantity of single strike options spread among different traders. However, these trades are not done exactly simultaneously. Traders who trade the last of a large lot order will find themselves at a competitive disadvantage when attempting to complete delta futures hedges because the impact on futures prices will already have been caused by the delta hedging of the first of the serial traders. What was a large profit for the first traders to do a string trade turns into a large loss for the last of the string traders, after futures prices have been run up or down by the first traders doing their futures hedges. Trading last on a string should be avoided whenever possible.

Overtrading

Another common mistake of option traders is overtrading, or impatience. Some market makers may get so bored from too much inactivity or not participating in trades that trades are done at net fair value. The market maker is not waiting for a sufficient edge to trade. Overtrading is unnecessary, and it may be wasteful if losses accrue because the profit margin is too thin.

A market maker should not look to trade all trades being done in the pit, but only to trade those at his prices. Of all trades done in the pit, there will be some minority of trades done at excessive discounts or premiums to fair value. Good option trading is waiting for these trades during the day, and not overtrading. There is no virtue in being the most active trader, only the most profitable. A good trader must be patient.

Poor Kappa (K)/Vega Risk Adjustment

A trader may become too long or short kappa/vega in context of the market liquidity on the opposite side. A trader does one side of an option trade repeatedly without a corresponding option spread trade. Even though the trader adjusts for delta neutrality, kappa/vega risk becomes lopsided. In the worst situation a trader has allowed a negative kappa/vega position to develop. This should always be corrected immediately.

The rule of thumb is to remain net long kappa/vega but not to get net kappa/vega more than may be neutralized without too large a loss if necessary. This amount is sometimes difficult to determine in practice and may be a judgment call in which errors will inevitably occur. To a considerable extent, judgment will be based on the trader's appraisal of the net flow of pit/broker option trading.

Other Mistakes

One should also appreciate that clerical errors (mistakes in quantity, strike, month, or side) do occur, and they are truly inevitable. Perhaps one in 20 times, a small error is made. These are a cost of doing business and should be looked at philosophically.

More generally, traders will be making a mistake if they do not learn to relax during the trading day and take vacations periodically. One of the advantages of trading limited-risk carryover positions is that a trader never needs to worry about financial catastrophe happening to him or her and may sleep restfully at night.

Periodic vacations are also in order, and may be conveniently arranged to begin after some expiration. Even if a trader does not liquidate his or her entire position, it is possible with planning to reduce position gamma to very low levels so that one need not be in daily contact with the market.

9

Observations from the Floor

There [on the exchange floor], 50 or 60 grown men stood leaning in each others' faces shouting as loudly as they could in primordial tones of voice that I had never heard before, except maybe the one time I tried to take a shrimp away from my cat, Paco. Veins bulged in the men's necks. Their eyes seemed ready to leap from their sockets at any moment. They waved their arms threateningly at one another in some incomprehensible code.

It was like a cockfight without the cocks. A crowd this angry couldn't help but come to blows at any moment.... My heart was in my throat. What was going on here?

The men were trading cotton.

Albert Pacelli, 1991

A first-time visitor to any major commodity exchange will see a horde of screaming, elbowing traders packed densely into an open space as big as a sports stadium, while a deafening roar painfully presses the eardrums. What is a homely workplace to some would count as Dante's Seventh Circle of Hell to most. Recently, several books reported for the first time on the strange rituals of exchange floor social and professional life (Tamarkin, 1985; Kleinfield, 1983; Marks, 1988).

Becoming a good option scalper requires several skills and assets. Good options trading is preeminently a numbers game and requires a good numbers sense. An ability to do quick calculations repetitively, sometimes in one's head, is a distinct advantage. Option traders frequently enjoy playing number games (bridge, chess, go, poker) and are good at them, although few seem interested in gambling outside of work aside from occasional small but popular informal sports pools.

Physical stamina and the reflexes of an athlete may be just as important as good mathematical intelligence, for floor traders work in a harsh physical and personal environment where competition is intense. Self-esteem is also necessary, for new as well as old traders are likely to suffer direct personal insults on a regular basis or discouragements from other traders who would like to minimize competition. Traders are not known for keeping their voices down or using polite language when they are verbally abusing another trader, fines notwithstanding. There is always someone in any crowd who has difficulty mastering maturity, although the worst offender is likely to be different for each person. Trading pit manners are often nasty, brutish and loud. A new trader must have sufficient self-esteem and perseverance to withstand this kind of occasional psychological warfare and not let himself become emotionally involved.

Correspondingly, a strong cooperative style is a plus, because trading involves being on good terms daily with many traders, brokers, and support staff. Many option traders are partners in option partnerships and must work cooperatively with other partners in a high-stress environment. Traders with bad tempers or those who are unwilling to compromise frequently do not have good floor reputations and risk losing business in the long run.

A sound sense of business conduct and morals must also be considered an important virtue. Most exchanges now require new members to take an ethics course, conducted by lawyers and surveillance officials, that stresses the serious consequences awaiting a trader who breaks the rules. Although the overwhelming majority of floor traders are scrupulously honest, floor traders may eventually encounter some individuals or situations where violating exchange rules may result in some unethical or illegal profit. Unethical and fraudulent traders, however, will almost always be discovered over a lifetime and suffer large fines or expulsion, as they should in every profession.

The professional path of market makers is likely to be varied, and there are several ways to start on this career. For *upstairs* market making in electronic screen-traded over-the-counter financial options, market makers are employees or partners of large investment banks, international banks, or other trading firms, and often start as clerks or assistant traders. Market makers on option exchanges are sometimes regulated specialists, as in stock options, or may be independent traders trading for a partnership or their own account.

Capitalization of many of the independent market makers is relatively small. Current full memberships on futures and option exchanges in the United States range from $1,000 to $500,000 (with the New York Futures Exchange probably the lowest, and the Chicago Mercantile Exchange the highest). Other memberships, including special option memberships, may be almost anywhere between those two extremes, although perhaps half of all option memberships in the United States are under $50,000. Sometimes option memberships may be leased, with leases currently running from 1 to 2 percent of option seat value per month. In addition to seat capitalization, option market making requires liquid capital to meet basic margin requirements. This is hardly ever less than $25–50,000 as a minimum. For over-the-counter option markets, capital requirements may be significantly higher to handle large institutional trading.

The 1980s was the second decade of continued strong growth of option trading in the United States. This has been the spur to the expansion of option markets. European and Asian option markets are following the growth path of the United States, promising that the 1990s will be the third consecutive decade of growth in world option markets. Many of these new markets may prove to be among the best option markets for market makers.

John Maynard Keynes once called trading a game. If this is true, it may not be whether one wins or loses that counts, but whether one ever ventures to play. For those who do, good luck.

Appendix

Option Software for Market Making

To keep track of the risks and profitability of large option positions it is almost always necessary to use an option analysis computer software program. Although hand calculations are not impossible, a computer can evaluate instantaneously a constantly changing option position over a number of risk assumptions. Also, software is indispensable for printing fair-value sheets upon which market-maker quotations are based.

Listed below are some option software vendors who appeal to option dealers and market makers. Listing in this Appendix does not imply endorsement of services but is provided for informational purposes only.

TRACK DATA
The Option Group (TOG)
61 Broadway Suite 2301
New York, NY 10006
212-943-4555

COMTEK
141 W. Jackson Blvd. Suite 1531-A
Chicago, IL 60604

EPSILON OPTIONS
Box 3207
Church St. Station
New York, NY 10102

OPTIONS AND ALTERNATIVES SOFTWARE
Chicago Mercantile Exchange Marketing Department
30 S. Wacker Dr.
Chicago, IL 60606
312-930-1000

REUTER SCHWARZATRON
61 Broadway
New York, NY 10006
212-493-7100

SYSTEMS DEVELOPMENT CORP.
RAMBO
141 W. Jackson Blvd. Suite 1240-A
Chicago, IL 60604
312-408-1111

OPTIONOMICS
3191 S. Valley St. Suite 155
Salt Lake City, UT 84109
1-800-255-3374

References and Suggested Reading

Baker, Wayne E. (1984). "Floor Trading and Crowd Dynamics." In Patricia A. Adler and Peter Adler (Eds.). *The Social Dynamics of Financial Markets.* Greenwich, CT: JAI Press.

Black, Fischer. (1976). "The Pricing of Commodity Contracts," *Journal of Financial Economics, 3.*

Black, Fischer, and Myron Scholes. (1973). "The Pricing of Options and Corporate Liabilities," *Journal of Political Economy*, May/June.

Bobin, Christopher A. (1990). *Agricultural Options: Trading, Risk, and Management.* New York: John Wiley & Sons.

Bookstaber, Richard M. (1987). *Option Pricing and Investment Strategies.* Chicago: Probus.

Brealey, Richard A. (1969). *An Introduction to Risk and Return from Common Stocks.* Cambridge, MA: MIT Press.

Chicago Board Options Exchange (Ed.). (1990). *Options: Essential Concepts and Trading Strategies.* Homewood, IL: Business One Irwin.

Chicago Board of Trade (1989). *Commodity Futures Professional.* January.

Colburn, James T. (1990). *Trading in Options on Futures.* New York: New York Institute of Finance.

Cootner, Paul (Ed.). (1964). *The Random Character of Stock Prices.* Cambridge MA: MIT Press.

Cox, John C., and Mark Rubinstein. (1985). *Option Markets.* Englewood Cliffs, NJ: Prentice-Hall.

Edwards, Robert, and John Magee. (1957). *Technical Analysis of Stock Trends*. Springfield MA: John Magee.

Gastineau, Gary. (1979/1988). *Stock Options Manual*. New York: McGraw-Hill.

Gehm, Fred. (1983). *Commodity Market Money Management*. New York: John Wiley & Sons.

Goss, Barry A. (1986). *Futures Markets: Their Establishment and Performance*. New York: New York University Press.

Greene, Mark R. (1962). *Risk and Insurance*. Cincinnati, OH: South-Western Publishing.

Hagin, Robert. (1979). *The Dow Jones-Irwin Guide to Modern Portfolio Theory*. Homewood, IL: Dow Jones-Irwin.

Hastings, N. A. J. and J. B. Peacock. (1975). *Statistical Distributions*. London: Butterworth.

Henriques, Diana. (1988, November 28). "Scrumptious Spread: Arbs Take a Shine to the Silver Market." *Barron's*.

Horn, Frederick F., and Victor Farah. (1979). *Trading Commodity Futures* (2nd ed.). New York: New York Institute of Finance.

Kaufman, Perry J. (1987). *The New Commodity Trading Systems and Methods*. New York: John Wiley & Sons.

Kleinfield, Sonny. (1983). *The Traders*. New York: Holt, Rinehart & Winston.

Labuszewski, John, and Jeanne Cairns Sinquefield. (1988). *Inside the Commodity Option Markets*. New York: John Wiley & Sons.

London Metal Exchange. (1988). *The London Metal Exchange*. Tonbridge, England: Whitefriars Press.

Maddala, G. S., and Jisoo Yoo. (1990) "Risk Premia and Price Volatility in Futures Markets," Center for the Study of Futures Markets, Columbia University, Working Paper #205, Fall.

Mandelbrot, B. (1964) "The Variation of Certain Speculative Prices." In P. Cootner (Ed.), *The Random Character of Stock Prices*. Cambridge, MA: MIT Press.

Marks, Janet Rose. (1988). Disguise and Display: Balancing Profit and Morality in the Pit of a Commodities Futures Exchange (Doctoral Dissertation, New York University).

McMillan, Lawrence. (1986). *Options as a Strategic Investment*, New York: Prentice Hall.

Merton, Robert. (1973). "Theory of Rational Option Pricing,"*Bell Journal of Economics and Management Science*, **4,** Spring.

Natanberg, Sheldon. (1988). *Option Volatility and Pricing Strategies*. Chicago: Probus.

Nelson, Ray D. (1988). "Exploring the Shapes of Probability Densities for Chicago Board of Trade September Wheat Futures Price Change," Center for the Study of Futures Markets, Columbia University, Working Paper #175. August.

New York Times (1989, October 18). "Stock Slide Forces Closing of Chicago Options Firm."

Pacelli, Albert Peter. (1991). *The Speculator's Edge*. New York: John Wiley & Sons.

Peters, Edgar E. (1991). *Chaos and Order in the Capital Markets*. New York: John Wiley & Sons.

Olkin, Ingram, and Leon J. Gleser, and Cyrus Derman. (1980). *Probability Models and Applications*. New York: Macmillan.

Options Clearing Corporation. (1987). *Characteristics and Risks of Standardized Options*. Chicago: Author.

Reichenstein, William, and Wallace Davidson III. (1987, September 14). "Sporting Chances: Comparing Options and Football Bets," *Barron's*.

Sarnoff, Paul. (1967). *Jesse Livermore: Speculator-King*. Greenville, SC: Trader's Press.

Schwager, Jack D. (1989). *Market Wizards: Interviews with Top Traders*. New York: New York Institute of Finance.

Siconolfi, Michael. (1990, November 12). "Volume Investors Case Finally Closes," Wall Street Journal.

Silber, William. (1984). "Marketmaker Behavior in an Auction Market: An Analysis of Scalpers in Futures Markets," Journal of Finance **39** (4), September.

_____ (1988). "Market Making in Options: Principles and Implications," in *Salomon Brothers Center Proceedings,* New York University, December.

Smith, Adam. (1969). *Money Game*. New York: Dell.

Sterge, A. J. (1989). "On the Distribution of Financial Futures Price Changes," *Financial Analysts Journal,* May/June.

Stoll, Hans R. (1987). "The Economics of Market Making." In *NASDAQ Handbook,* National Association of Securities Dealers, Chicago: Probus.

Tamarkin, Bob. (1985). *The New Gatsbys: Fortunes and Misfortunes of Commodity Traders.* New York: William Morrow & Co.

Teweles, Richard, and Frank J. Jones. (1987). *The Futures Game: Who Wins? Who Loses? Why?* New York: McGraw-Hill.

Tomek, William G, and Kenneth L. Robinson. (1972). *Agricultural Product Prices.* Ithaca, NY: Cornell University Press.

Turner, A. L. and E. J. Weigel. (1990). "An Analysis of Stock Market Volatility," in *Russell Research Commentaries.* Tacoma, WA: Frank Russell Co.

Wall Street Journal (1987, October 13). "Trader Involved in Big Losses Identified."

_____ (1991, January 28). "Commodity Trading Advice Shouldn't Be Taken To the Letter."

Williams, Jeffrey. (1986). *The Economic Function of Futures Markets.* London: Cambridge University Press.

Wolff, Rudolf (1987). *Wolff's Guide to the London Metal Exchange.* Surrey, England: Metal Bulletin Books Ltd.

Wong, M. Anthony. (1991). *Trading and Investing in Bond Options: Risk Management, Arbitrage, and Value Investing.* New York: John Wiley & Sons.

Working, Holbrook. (1977). "Tests of a Theory Concerning Floor Trading on a Commodity Exchange," Selected Writings, Chicago Board of Trade.

Index

Printed and bound by CPI Group (UK) Ltd, Croydon, CR0 4YY

24/04/2025

14661360-0001